basix Guitar Chord Dictionary

D1316488

Photos courtesy of Gibson Guitar
Les Paul Standard, Heritage Cherry Sunburst
Chet Atkins CE, Antique Natural

Alfred

Play any note on the guitar, then play a note one fret above it. The distance between these two notes is a *half step*. Play another note followed by a note two frets above it. The distance between these two notes is a *whole step* (two half steps). The distance between any two notes is referred to as an *interval*.

In the example of the C major scale below, the letter names are shown above the notes and the *scale degrees* (numbers) of the notes are written below. Notice that C is the first degree of the scale, D is the second, etc.

The name of an interval is determined by counting the number of scale degrees from one note to the next. For example: An interval of a 3rd, starting on C, would be determined by counting up three scale degrees, or C-D-E (1-2-3). C to E is a 3rd. An interval of a 4th, starting on C, would be determined by counting up four scale degrees, or C-D-E-F (1-2-3-4). C to F is a 4th.

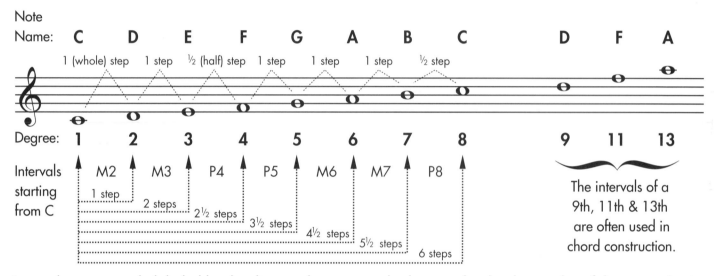

Intervals are not only labeled by the distance between scale degrees, but by the *quality* of the interval. An interval's quality is determined by counting the number of whole steps and half steps between the two notes of an interval. For example: C to E is a 3rd. C to E is also a major third because there are 2 whole steps between C and E. Likewise, C to E♭ is a 3rd. C to E♭ is also a minor third because there are 1½ steps between C and E♭. There are five qualities used to describe intervals: *major, minor, perfect, diminished and augmented.*

Sting

M	=	Major	o	=	Diminished (dim)
m	=	minor	+	=	Augmented (aug)
P	=	Perfect			

Particular intervals are associated with certain qualities:

2nds, 9ths	=	Major, Minor & Augmented
3rds, 6ths, 13ths	=	Major, Minor, Augmented & Diminished
4ths, 5ths, 11ths	=	Perfect, Augmented & Diminished
7ths	=	Major, Minor & Diminished

Whether fronting the 1980s supergroup The Police *or exploring his own brand of jazz-infused pop music as a solo artist,* **Sting** *has always been an adventurous, highly-innovative artist.*

Intervals

When a *major* interval is made **smaller** by a half step it becomes a *minor* interval.

When a *minor* interval is made **larger** by a half step it becomes a *major* interval.

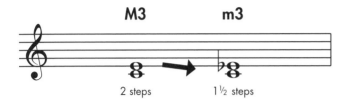

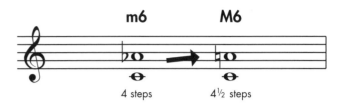

When a *minor* or *perfect* interval is made **smaller** by a half step it becomes a *diminished* interval.

When a *major* or *perfect* interval is made **larger** by a half step it becomes an *augmented* interval.

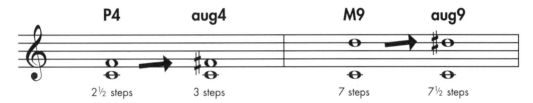

Below is a Table of Intervals starting on the note C. Notice that some intervals are labeled *enharmonic*, which means that they are written differently but sound the same (see **aug2** & **m3**).

TABLE OF INTERVALS

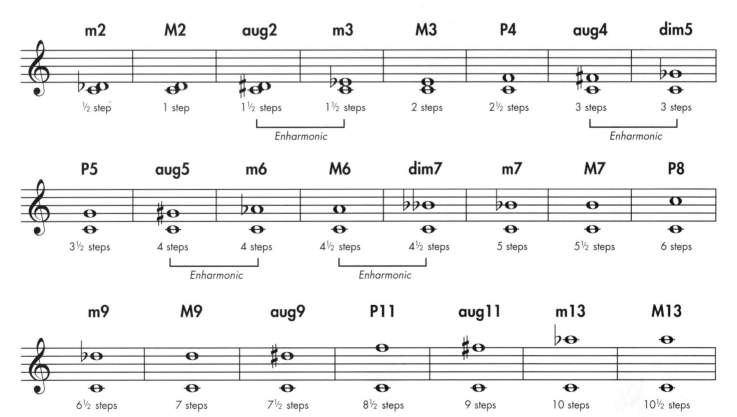

CHORD THEORY

Two or more notes played together is called a *chord*. Most commonly, a chord will consist of three or more notes. A three-note chord is called a *triad*. The *root* of a triad (or any other chord) is the note from which a chord is constructed. The relationship of the intervals from the root to the other notes of a chord determines the *chord type.* Triads are most frequently identified by four chord types: *major, minor, diminished and augmented.*

All chord types can be identified by the intervals used to create the chord. For example; the C major triad is built beginning with C as the root, adding a major 3rd (E) and adding a perfect 5th (G). All major triads contain a root, M3 and P5.

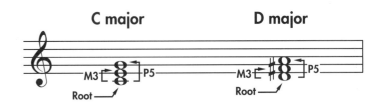

Minor triads contain a root, minor 3rd and perfect 5th. (An easier way to build a minor triad is to simply lower the 3rd of a major triad.) All minor triads contain a root, m3 and P5.

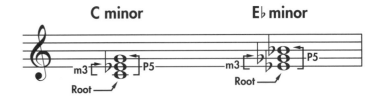

Diminished triads contain a root, minor 3rd and diminished 5th. If the perfect 5th of a minor triad is made smaller by a half step (to become a diminished 5th), the result is a diminished triad. All diminished triads contain a root, m3 and dim5.

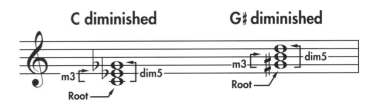

Augmented triads contain a root, major 3rd and augmented 5th. If the perfect 5th of a major triad is made larger by a half step (to become an augmented 5th), the result is an augmented triad. All augmented triads contain a root, M3 and aug5.

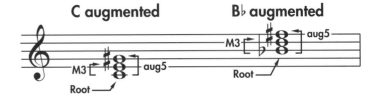

An important concept to remember about chords is that the bottom note of a chord will not always be the root. If the root of a triad, for instance, is moved above the 5th so that the 3rd is the bottom note of the chord, it is said to be in the *first inversion.* If the root and 3rd are moved above the 5th, the chord is in the *second inversion.* The number of inversions that a chord can have is related to the number of notes in the chord—a three-note chord can have two inversions, a four-note chord can have three inversions, etc.

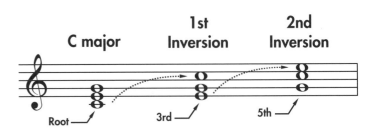

Building Chords

By using the four chord types as basic building blocks, it is possible to create a variety of chords by adding 6ths, 7ths, 9ths, 11ths, etc. The following are examples of some of the many variations:

* The *Suspended Fourth* chord does not contain a third. An assumption is made that the 4th degree of the chord will harmonically be inclined to *resolve* to the 3rd degree. In other words, the 4th is *suspended* until it moves to the 3rd.

CHORD THEORY

Thus far, the examples provided to illustrate intervals and chord construction have been based on C. Until familiarity with chords is achieved, the C chord examples on page 5 can serve as a reference guide when building chords based on other notes. For instance, locate C7(♭9) on page 5. To construct a G7(♭9) chord first determine what intervals are contained in C7(♭9) then follow the steps outlined below.

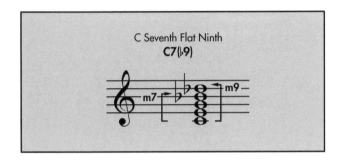

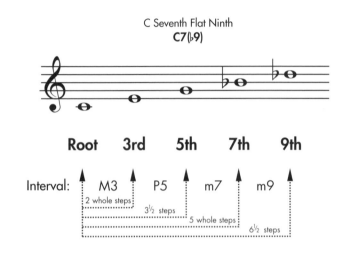

- Determine the *root* of the chord. A chord is always named for its root—in this instance, G is the root of G7(♭9).

- Count *letter names* up from the *letter name of the root* (G), as was done when building intervals on page 2, to determine the intervals of the chord. Therefore, counting 3 letter names up from G to B (G-A-B, 1-2-3) is a third, G to D (G-A-B-C-D) is a fifth, G to F is a seventh and G to A is a ninth.

- Determine the *quality* of the intervals by counting whole steps and half steps up from the root; G to B is a major 3rd (2 whole steps), G to D (3½ steps) is a perfect 5th, G to F (5 whole steps) is a minor seventh and G to A♭ (6½ steps) is a minor ninth.

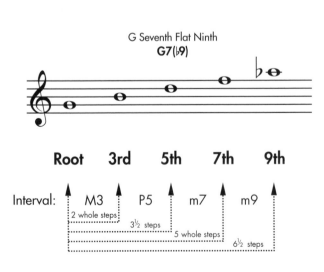

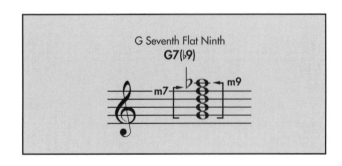

Follow this general guideline for determining the notes of any chord. As interval and chord construction become more familiar to the beginning guitarist, it will become possible to create original fingerings on the guitar. Experimentation is suggested.

Circle of Fifths

BASIX™ Guitar Chord Dictionary is organized to provide the fingerings of chords in all keys. The *Circle of Fifths* will help to clarify which chords are enharmonic equivalents (notice that *chords* can be written enharmonically as well as *notes*—see page 3). The Circle of Fifths also serves as a quick reference guide to the relationship of the keys and how key signatures can be figured out in a logical manner. Clockwise movement (up a P5) provides all of the sharp keys by adding one sharp to the key signature progressively. Counter-clockwise (down a P5) provides the flat keys by adding one flat similarly.

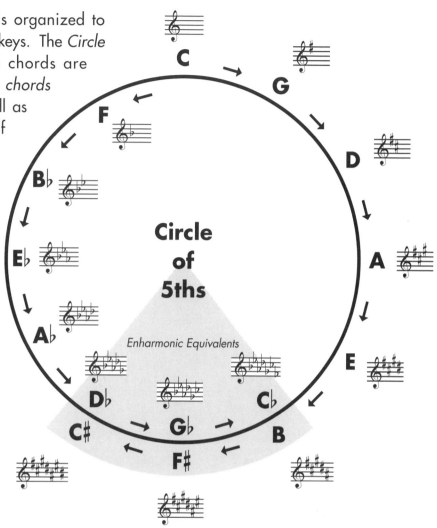

Circle
of
5ths

Enharmonic Equivalents

Elvis Costello started writing sophisticated, heartfelt tunes in the 1970s. His music has endured in part because of his willingness to explore many genres and styles.

Photo: Amy Lehman © 1995

Elvis Costello

READING CHORDS

Chord Symbol Variations

Chord symbols are a form of musical shorthand providing the guitarist with as much information about a chord as quickly as possible. The intent of using chord symbols is to convey enough information to recognize the chord yet not so much as to confuse the meaning of the symbol. Since chord symbols are not universally standardized, they are often written in many different ways—some are understandable, others are confusing. To illustrate this point, below is a listing of *some* of the ways copyists, composers and arrangers have created variations on the more common chord symbols:

C	**Csus**	**C($\flat$5)**	**C(add9)**	**C5**	**Cm**
C major	Csus4	C-5	C(9)	C(no3)	Cmin
Cmaj	C(addF)	C(5-)	C(add2)	C(omit3)	Cmi
CM	C4	C($\sharp$4)	C(+9)		C-
			C(+D)		

C+	**C°**	**C6**	**C6/9**	**Cm6/9**	**Cm6**
C+5	Cdim	Cmaj6	C6(add9)	C-6/9	C-6
Caug	Cdim7	C(addA)	C6(addD)	Cm6(+9)	Cm(addA)
Caug5	C7dim	C(A)	C9(no7)	Cm6(add9)	Cm(+6)
C($\sharp$5)			C9/6	Cm6(+D)	

C7	**C7sus**	**Cm7**	**Cm7($\flat$5)**	**C7+**	**C7($\flat$5)**
C(addB$\flat$)	C7sus4	Cmi7	Cmi7-5	C7+5	C7-5
C$\overline{7}$	Csus7	Cmin7	C-7(5-)	C7aug	C7(5-)
C(-7)	C7(+4)	C-7	C$\varnothing$	C7aug5	C$\overline{7}$-5
C(+7)		C7mi	C ½ dim	C7($\sharp$5)	C7($\sharp$4)

Cmaj7	**Cmaj7($\flat$5)**	**Cm(maj7)**	**C7($\flat$9)**	**C7($\sharp$9)**	**C7+($\flat$9)**
Cma7	Cmaj7(-5)	C-maj7	C7(-9)	C7(+9)	Caug7-9
C7	C$\overline{7}$(-5)	C-$\overline{7}$	C9$\flat$	C9$\sharp$	C+7($\flat$9)
C$\triangle$	C$\triangle$($\flat$5)	Cmi$\overline{7}$	C9-	C9+	C+9$\flat$
C$\triangle$7					C7+(-9)

Cm9	**C9**	**C9+**	**C9($\flat$5)**	**Cmaj9**	**C9($\sharp$11)**
Cm7(9)	C$^9_7$	C9(+5)	C9(-5)	C$\overline{7}$(9)	C9(+11)
Cm7(+9)	C7add9	Caug9	C7$^9_{-5}$	C$\overline{7}$(+9)	C($\sharp$11)
C-9	C7(addD)	C($\sharp$9$\sharp$5)	C9(5$\flat$)	C9(maj7)	C11+
Cmi7(9+)	C7(+9)	C+9		C$\overline{9}$	C11$\sharp$

Cm9(maj7)	**C11**	**Cm11**	**C13**	**C13($\flat$9)**	**C13($^{\flat 9}_{\flat 5}$)**
C-9($\sharp$7)	C9(11)	C-11	C9addA	C13(-9)	C13(-9-5)
C(-9)$\overline{7}$	C9addF	Cm($\flat$11)	C9(6)	C$\flat^{13}_9$	C($\flat$9$\flat$5)addA
Cmi9($\sharp$7)	C9+11	Cmi7$^{11}_9$	C7addA	C($\flat$9)addA	
	C7$^9_{11}$	C-7($^9_{11}$)	C7+A		

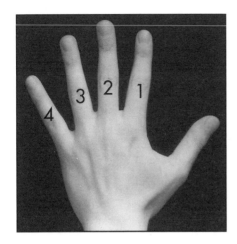

Guitar chord frames are diagrams that contain all the information necessary to play a particular chord. The fingerings, note names and position of the chord on the neck are all provided on the chord frame (see below). The photograph at left shows which finger number corresponds to which finger.

Choose chord positions that require the least motion from one chord to the next; select fingerings that are in approximately the same location on the guitar neck. This will provide smoother and more comfortable transitions between chords in a progression.

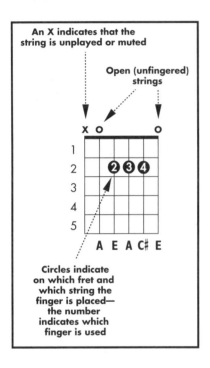

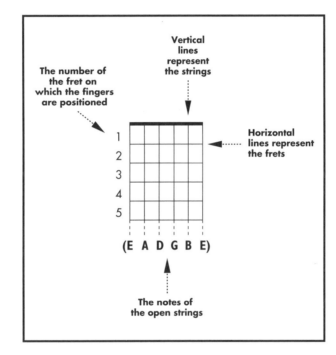

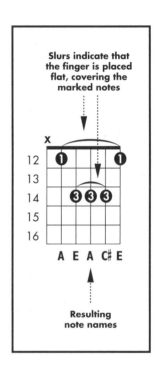

*Influenced by the guitar bands of the early 1980s New Wave movement, **Elastica** broke out of the British alternative scene in the mid-1990s to achieve commercial and critical success.*

Elastica

A♭

A♭	A♭sus	A♭(♭5)	A♭(add9)	A♭5	A♭m

Row 1:
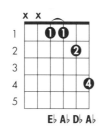 A♭ C E♭ A♭ C
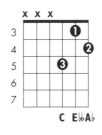 E♭ A♭ D♭ A♭
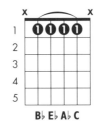 C E♭ A♭
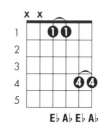 B♭ E♭ A♭ C
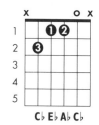 E♭ A♭ E♭ A♭
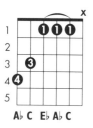 C♭ E♭ A♭ C♭

Row 2:
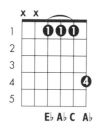 E♭ A♭ C A♭
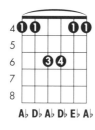 A♭ D♭ A♭ D♭ E♭ A♭
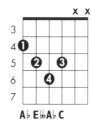 A♭ E♭ A♭ C
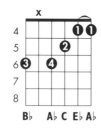 B♭ A♭ C E♭ A♭
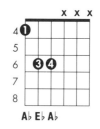 A♭ E♭ A♭
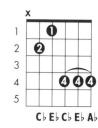 C♭ E♭ C♭ E♭ A♭

Row 3:
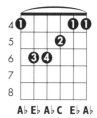 A♭ E♭ A♭ C E♭ A♭
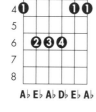 A♭ E♭ A♭ D♭ E♭ A♭
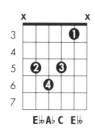 E♭ A♭ C E♭
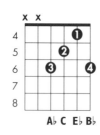 A♭ C E♭ B♭
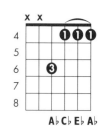 A♭ E♭ A♭ E♭ A♭
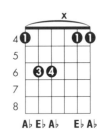 A♭ C♭ E♭ A♭

Row 4:
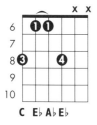 C E♭ A♭ E♭
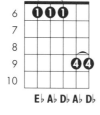 E♭ A♭ D♭ A♭ D♭
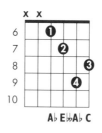 A♭ E♭ A♭ C
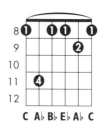 C A♭ B♭ E♭ A♭ C
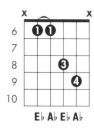 E♭ A♭ E♭ A♭
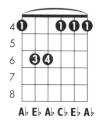 A♭ E♭ A♭ C♭ E♭ A♭

Row 5:
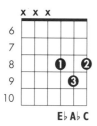 E♭ A♭ C
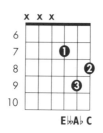 E♭ A♭ D♭
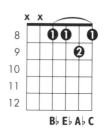 E♭ A♭ C
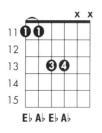 B♭ E♭ A♭ C
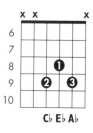 E♭ A♭ E♭ A♭
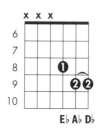 C♭ E♭ A♭

Row 6:
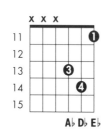 E♭ A♭ E♭ A♭ C E♭
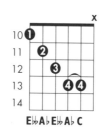 A♭ D♭ E♭
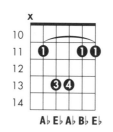 E♭ A♭ E♭ A♭ C
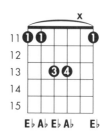 A♭ E♭ A♭ B♭ E♭
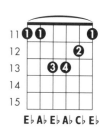 E♭ A♭ E♭ A♭ E♭
E♭ A♭ E♭ A♭ C♭ E♭

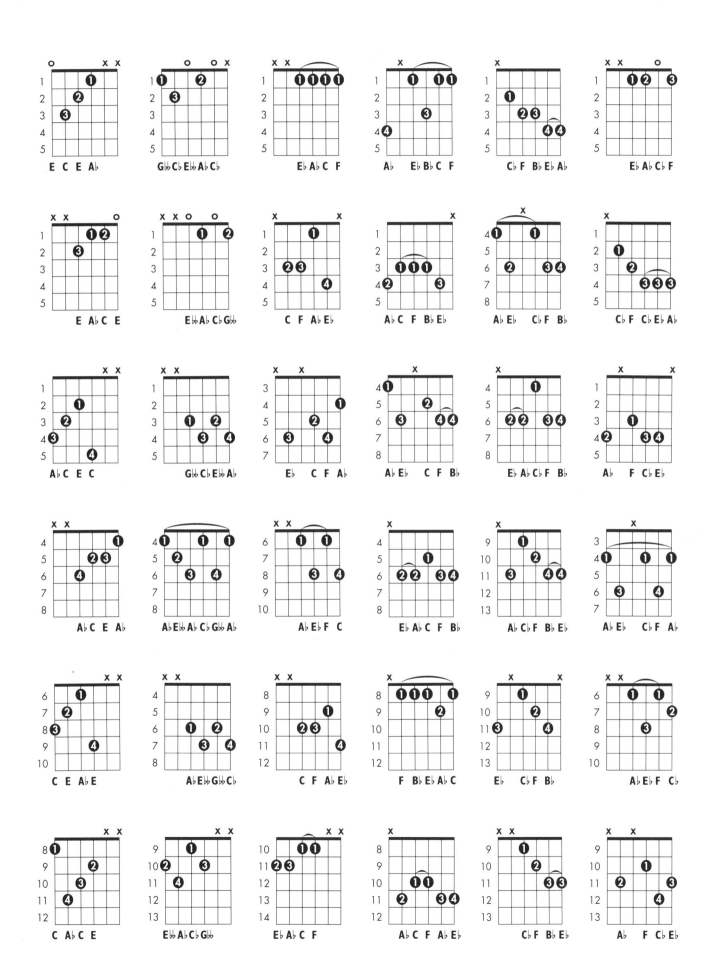

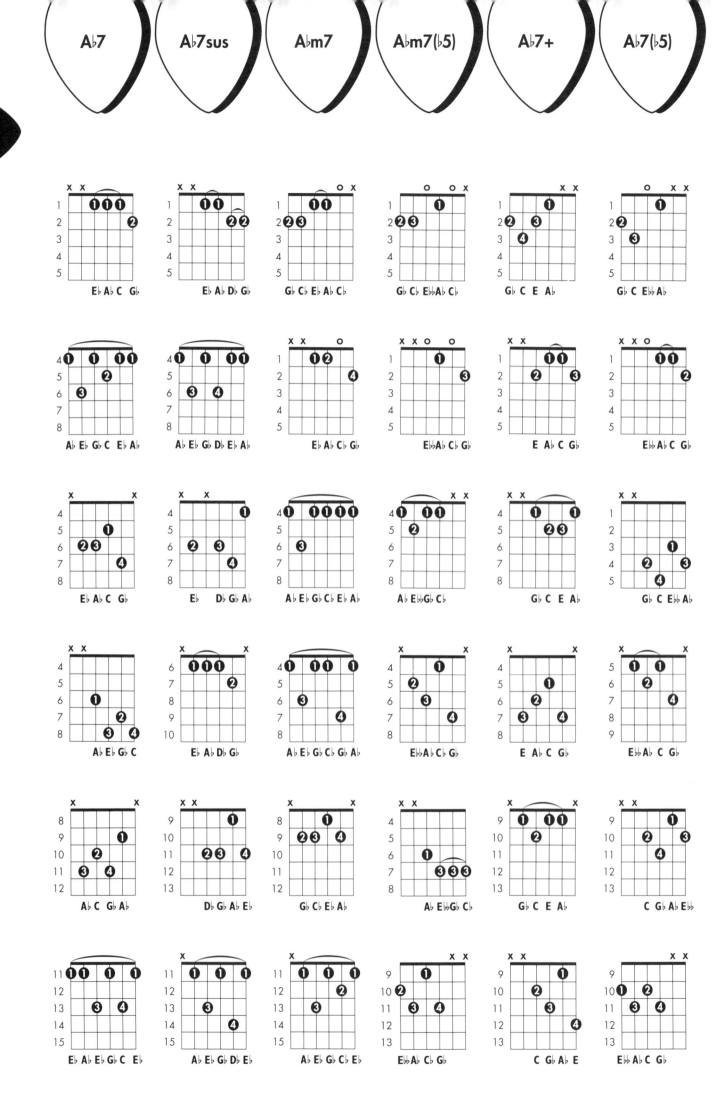

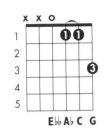

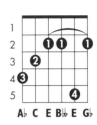

Abmaj7 Abmaj7(b5) Abm(maj7) Ab7(b9) Ab7(#9) Ab7+(b9)

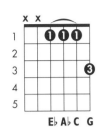
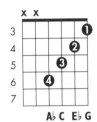
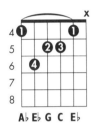
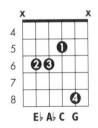
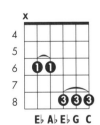
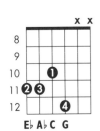

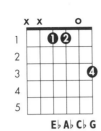
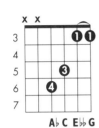
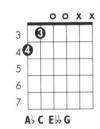
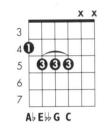
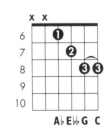
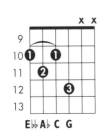

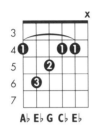
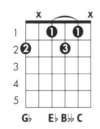
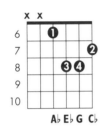
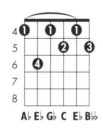
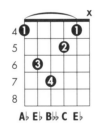
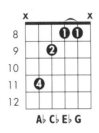
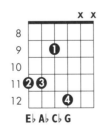
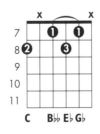
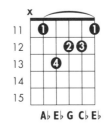
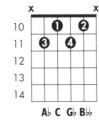

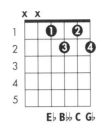
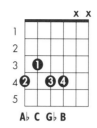
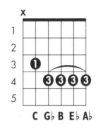
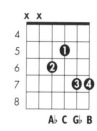
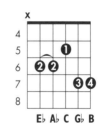
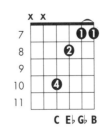

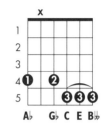
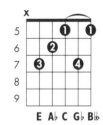
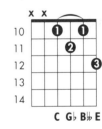

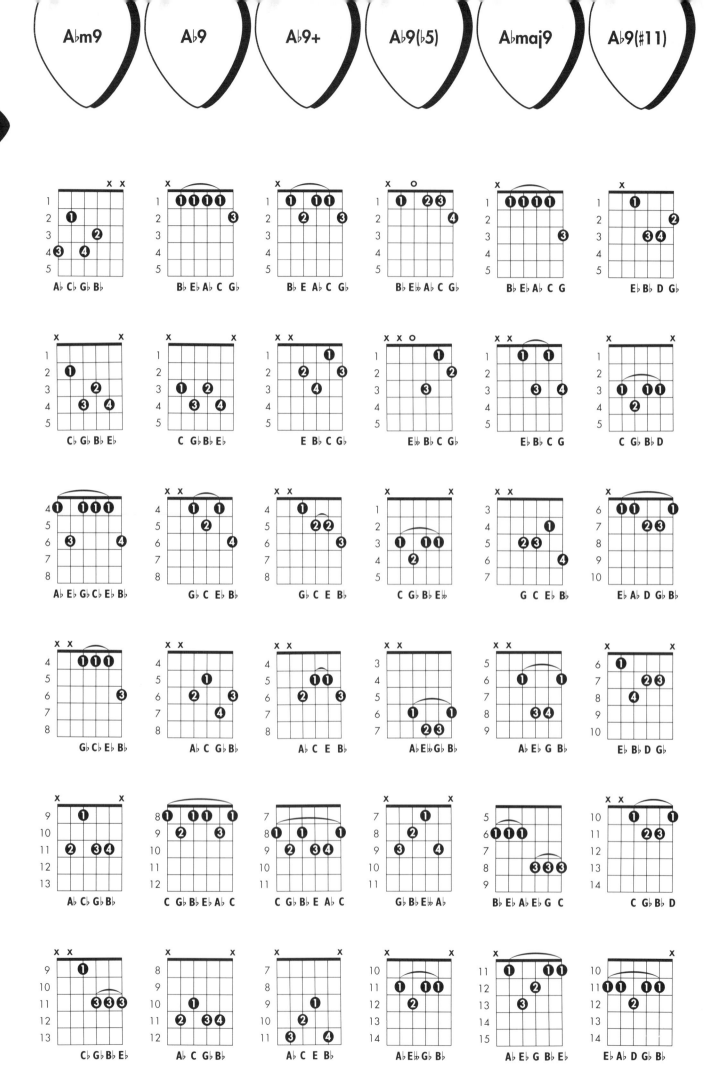

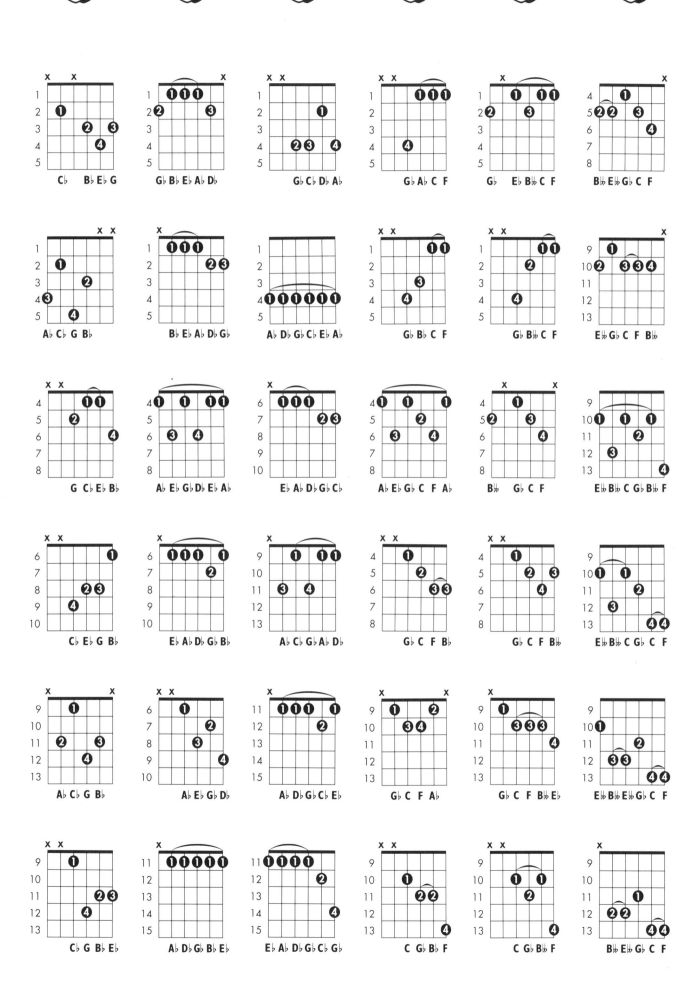

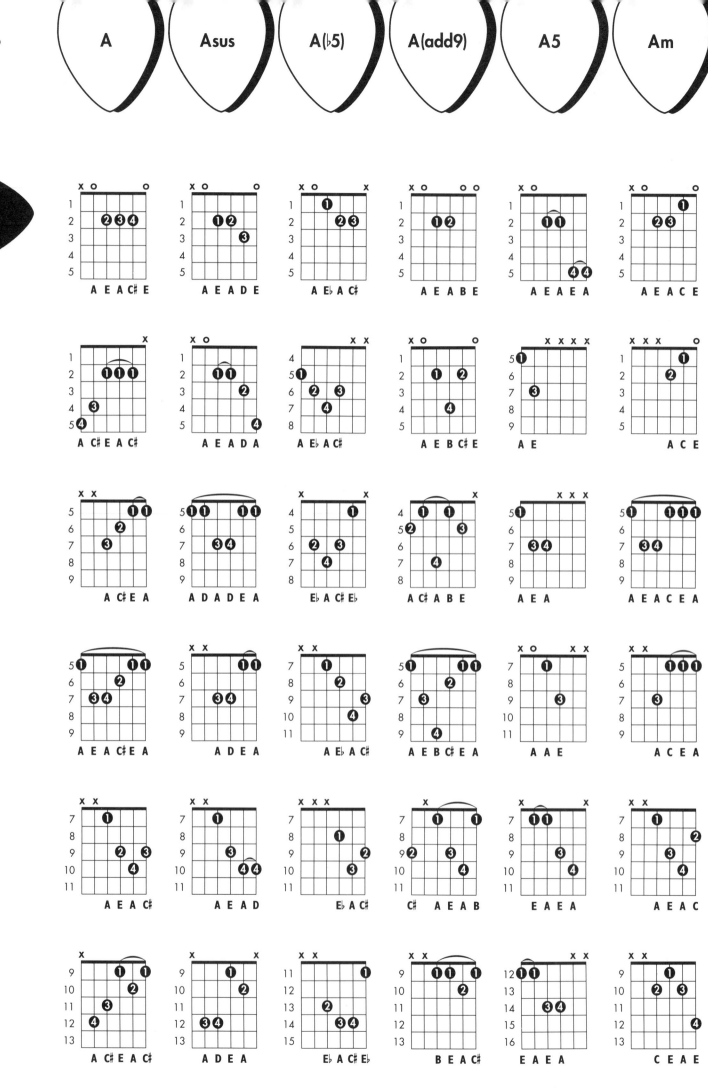

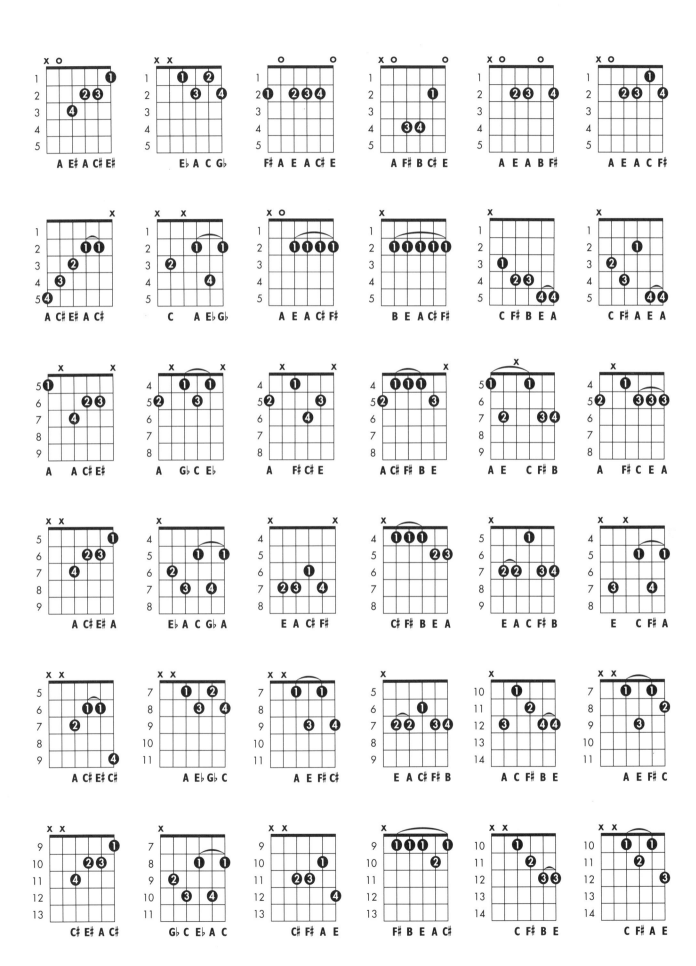

A+   A°   A6   A6/9   Am6/9   Am6

A

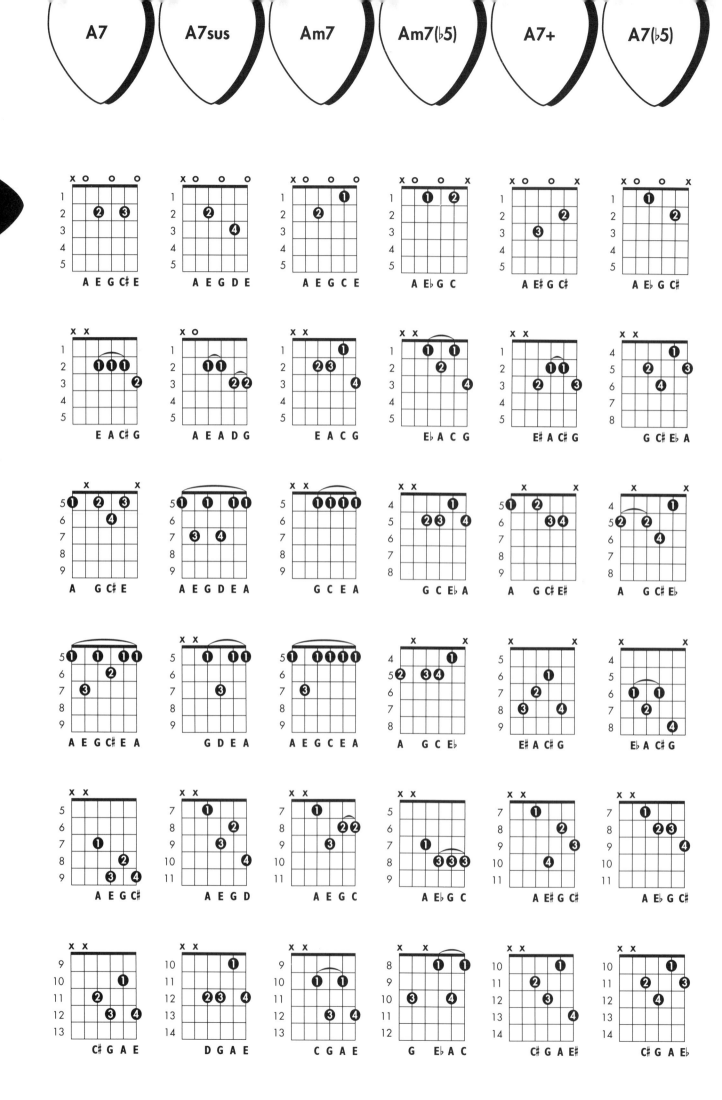

Amaj7   Amaj7(♭5)   Am(maj7)   A7(♭9)   A7(♯9)   A7+(♭9)

19

A

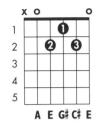 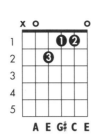 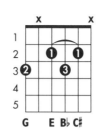 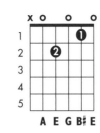 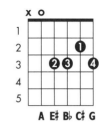 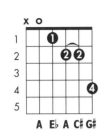

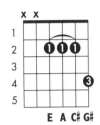 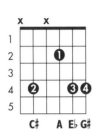 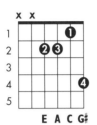 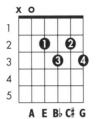 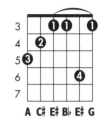 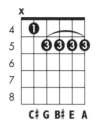

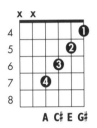 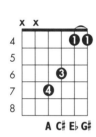 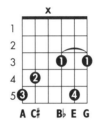 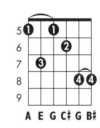 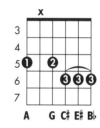 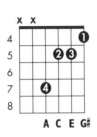

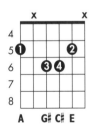 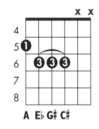 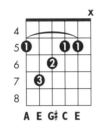 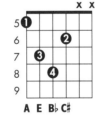 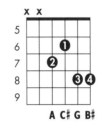 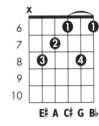

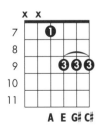 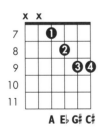 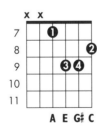 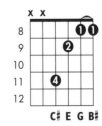 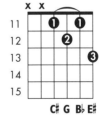 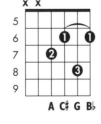

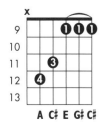 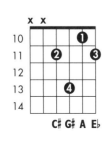 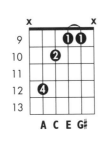 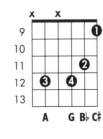 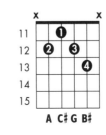 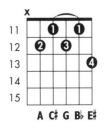

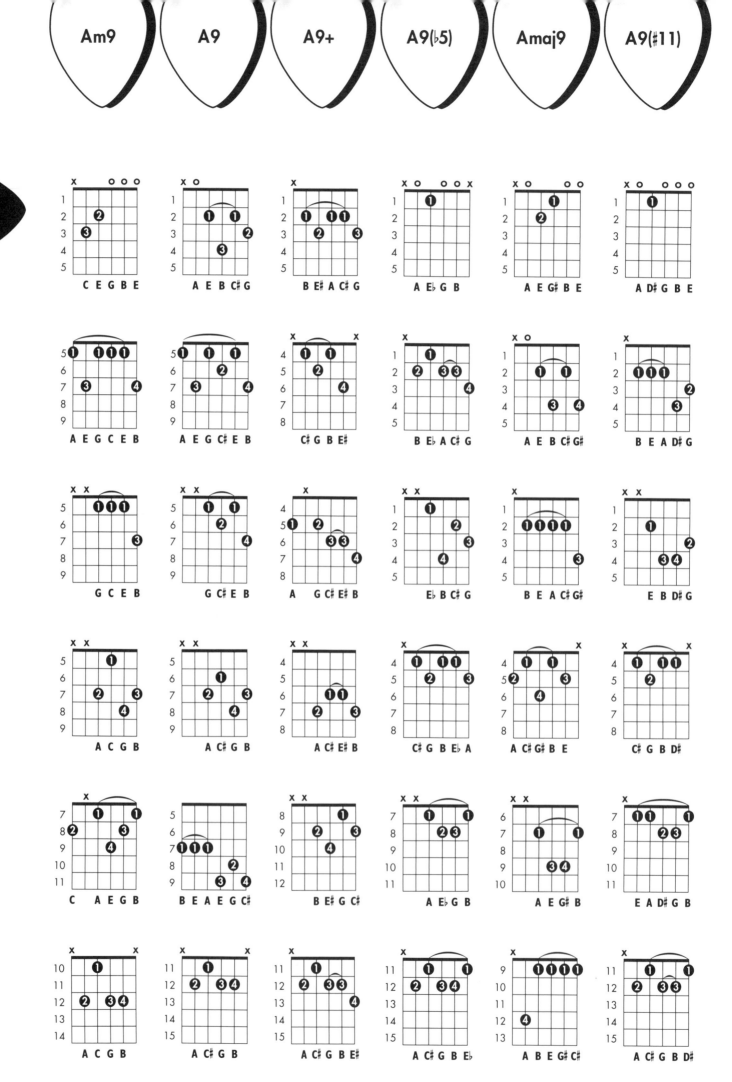

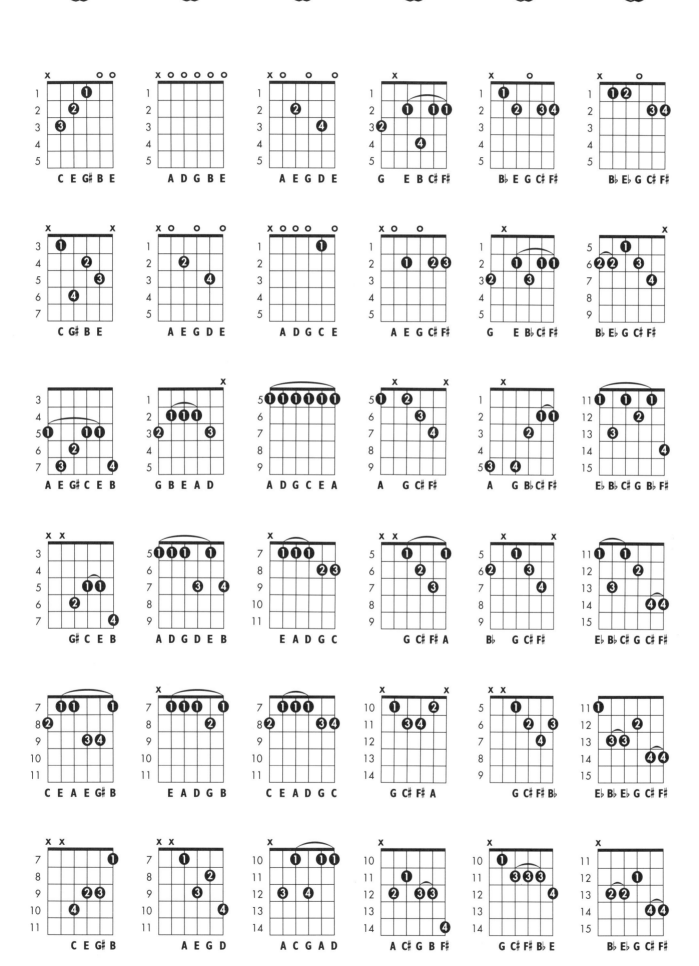

Am9(maj7)   A11   Am11   A13   A13(♭9)   A13(♭9♭5)

A

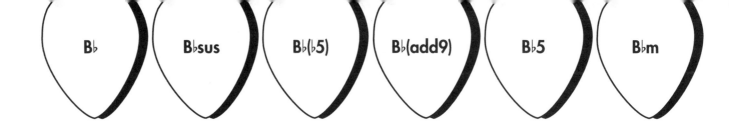

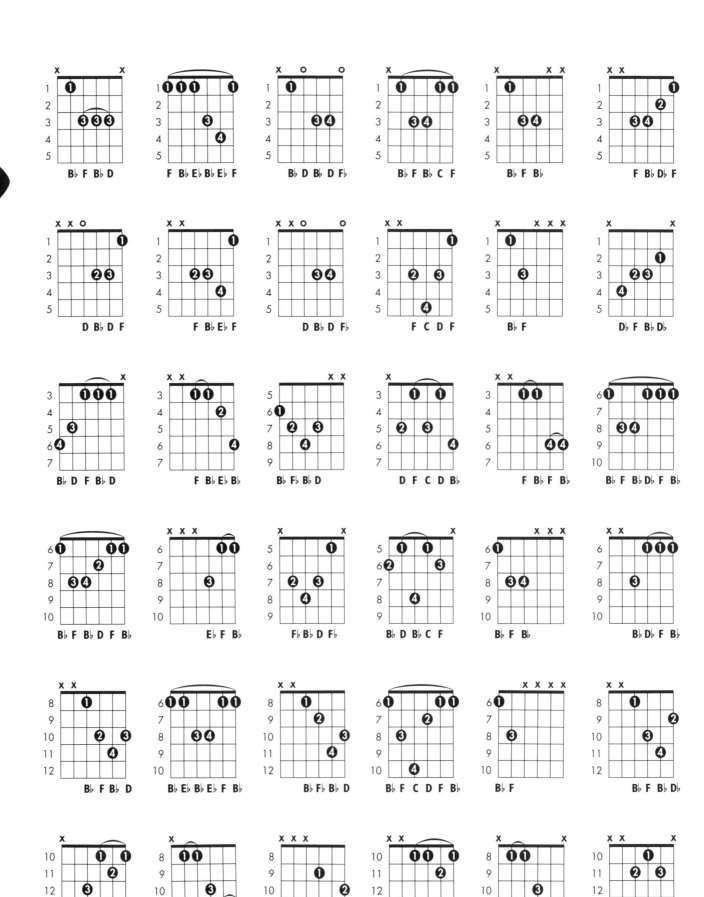

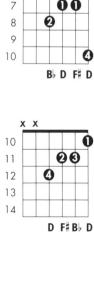

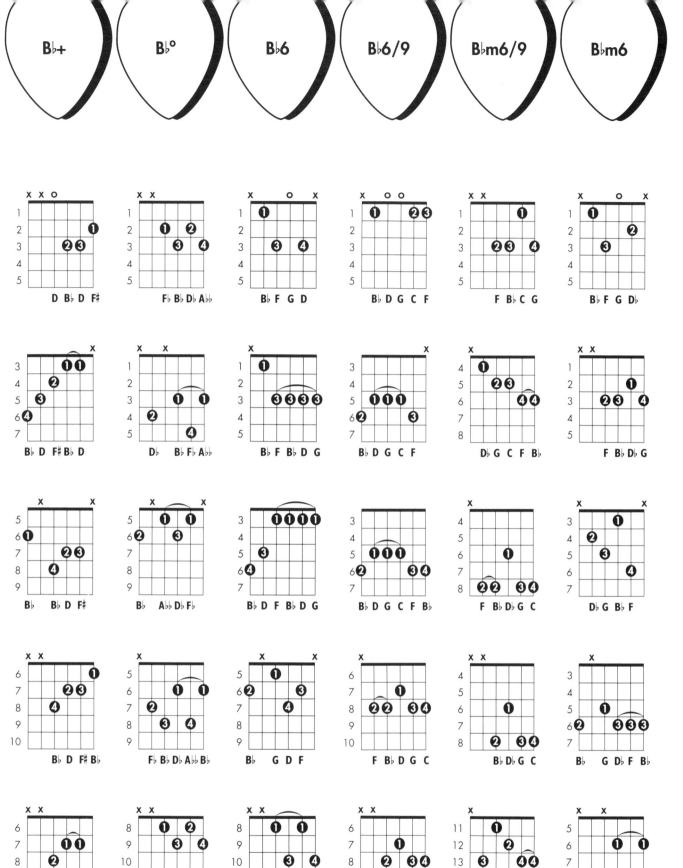

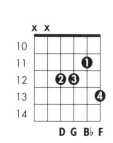

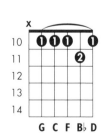

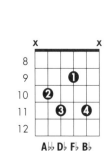

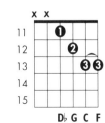

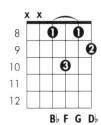

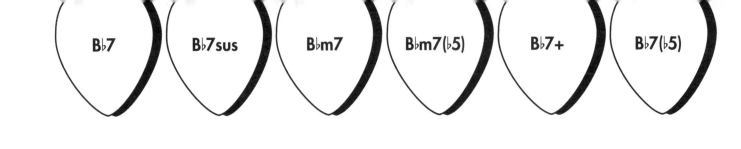

Bb7   Bb7sus   Bbm7   Bbm7(b5)   Bb7+   Bb7(b5)

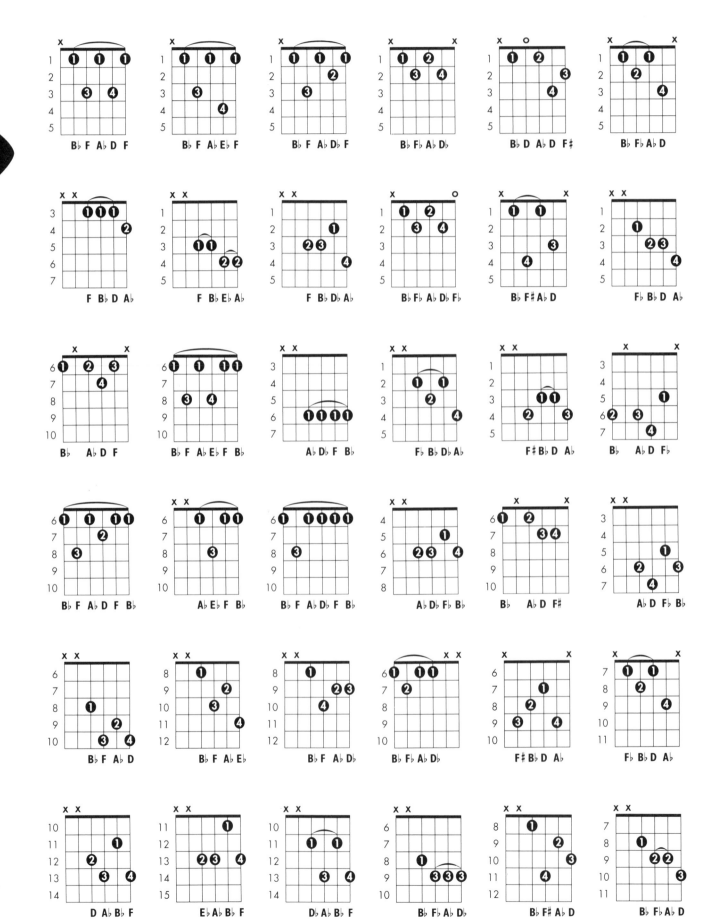

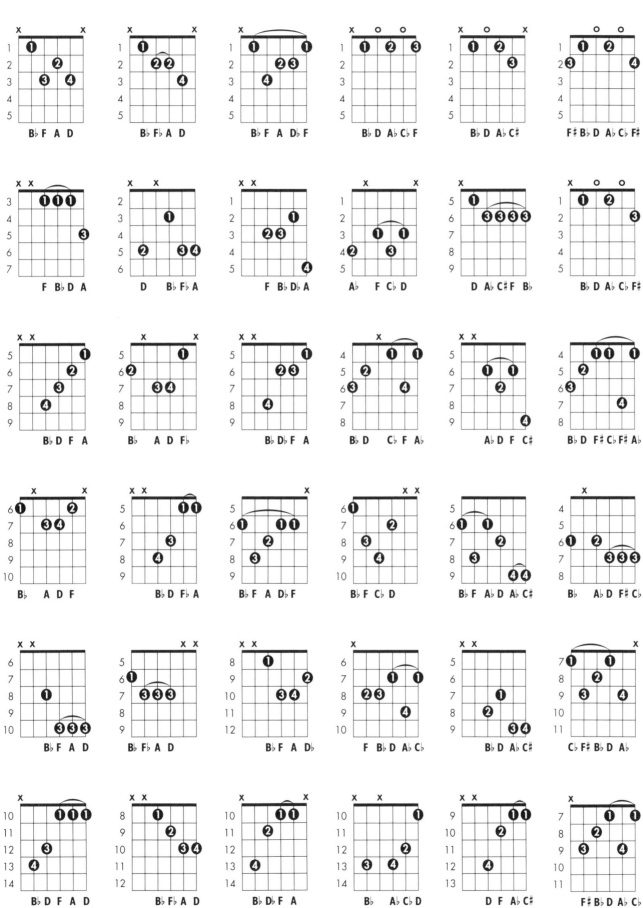

B♭maj7   B♭maj7(♭5)   B♭m(maj7)   B♭7(♭9)   B♭7(♯9)   B♭7+(♭9)

B♭

Bbm9 Bb9 Bb9+ Bb9(b5) Bbmaj9 Bb9(#11)

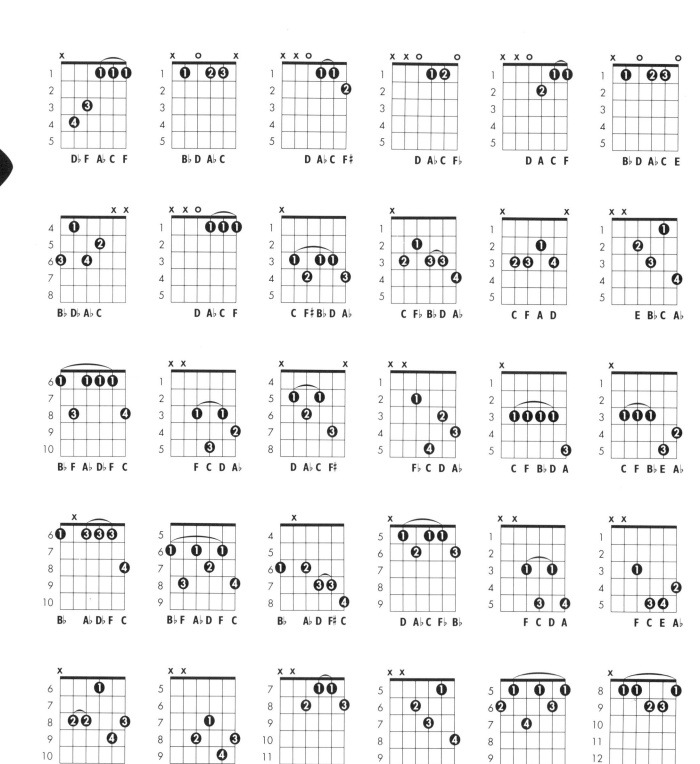

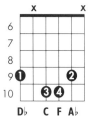
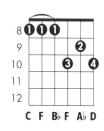
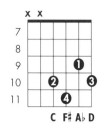
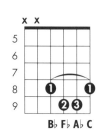
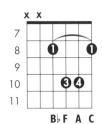

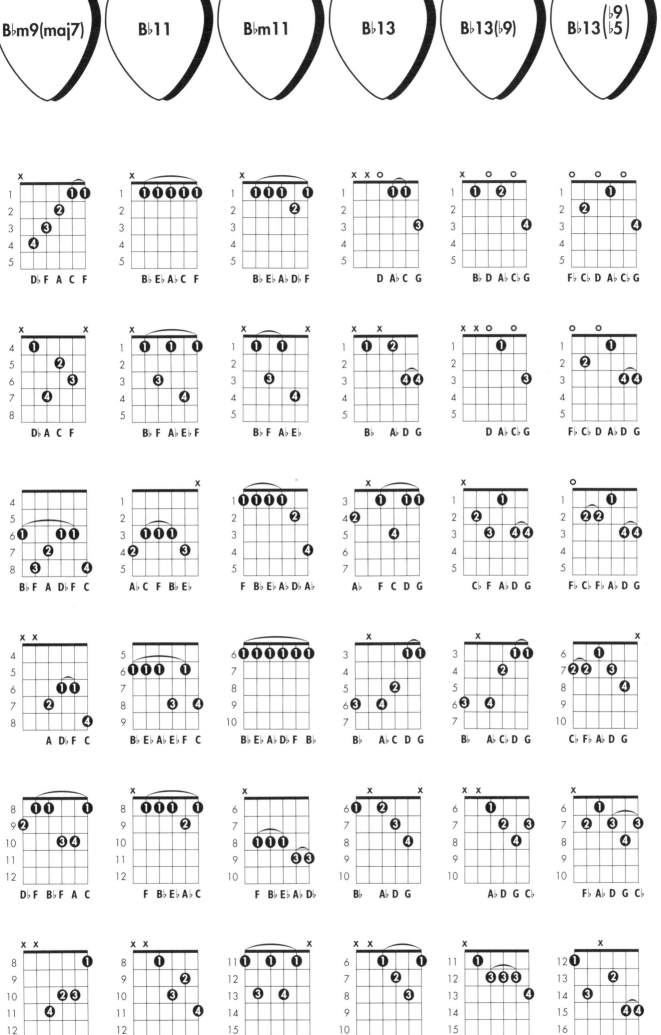

B♭m9(maj7) B♭11 B♭m11 B♭13 B♭13(♭9) B♭13($\begin{smallmatrix}♭9\\♭5\end{smallmatrix}$)

B♭

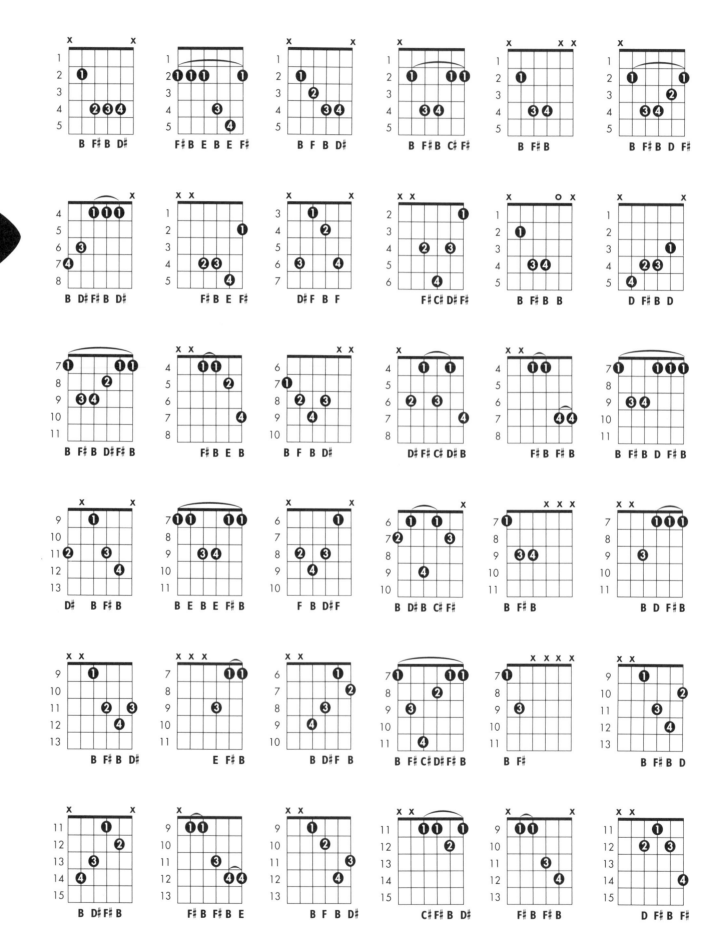

B   Bsus   B(♭5)   B(add9)   B5   Bm

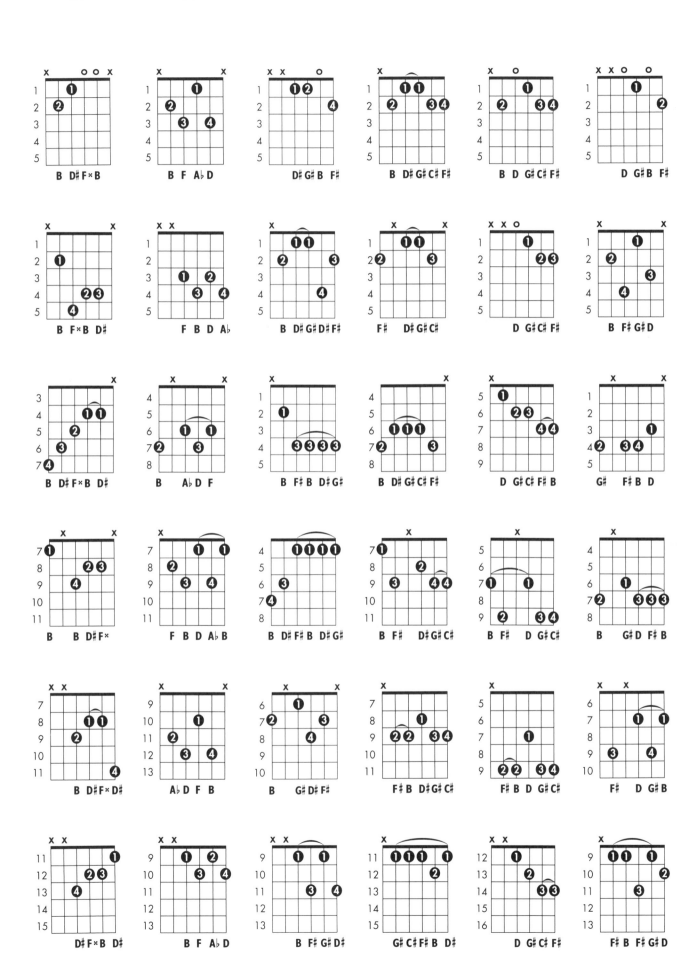

B+ B° B6 B6/9 Bm6/9 Bm6

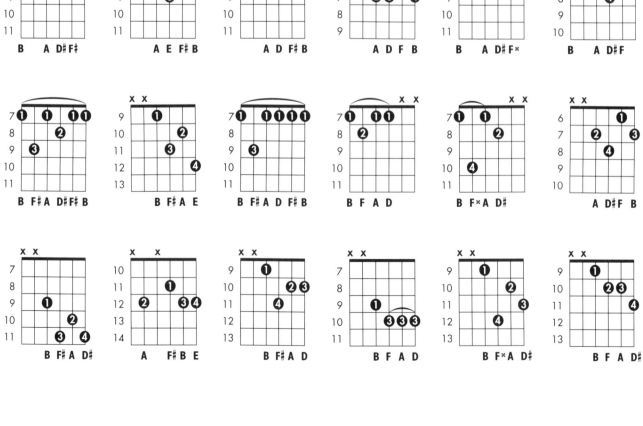

Bmaj7	Bmaj7(♭5)	Bm(maj7)	B7(♭9)	B7(♯9)	B7+(♭9)

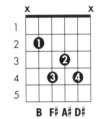 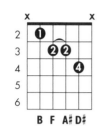 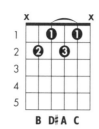 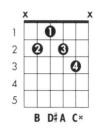 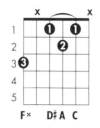 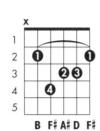

B F♯ A♯ D♯ | B F A♯ D♯ | B F♯A♯ D F♯ | B D♯A C | B D♯A C× | F× D♯A C

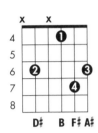 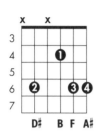 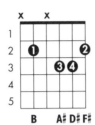 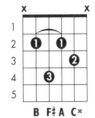 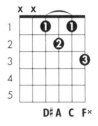 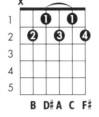

D♯ B F♯A♯ | D♯ B F A♯ | B A♯D♯F♯ | B D♯A C F♯ | B F♯A C× | D♯A C F×

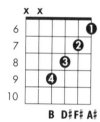 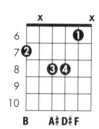 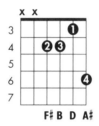 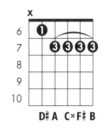 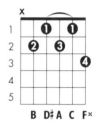 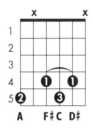

B D♯F♯ A♯ | B A♯D♯F | F♯B D A♯ | A F♯C D♯ | D♯A C×F♯ B | B D♯A C F×

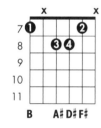 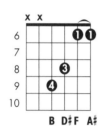 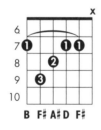 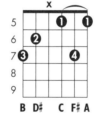 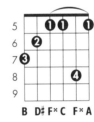 

B A♯D♯F♯ | B D♯F A♯ | B F♯A♯D F♯ | B D♯ C F♯A | A D♯F♯ C× | B D♯F×C F×A

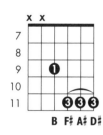 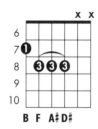 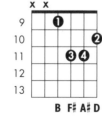 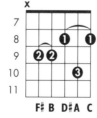 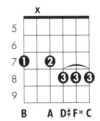 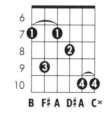

B F♯ A♯ D♯ | B F A♯D♯ | B F♯A♯ D | F♯B D♯A C | B F♯A D♯A C× | B A D♯F×C

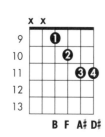 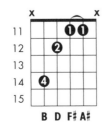 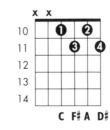 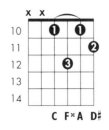 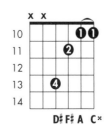

B D♯F♯A A♯ D♯ | B F A♯ D♯ | B D F♯A♯ | C F♯A D♯ | D♯F♯A C× | C F×A D♯

B

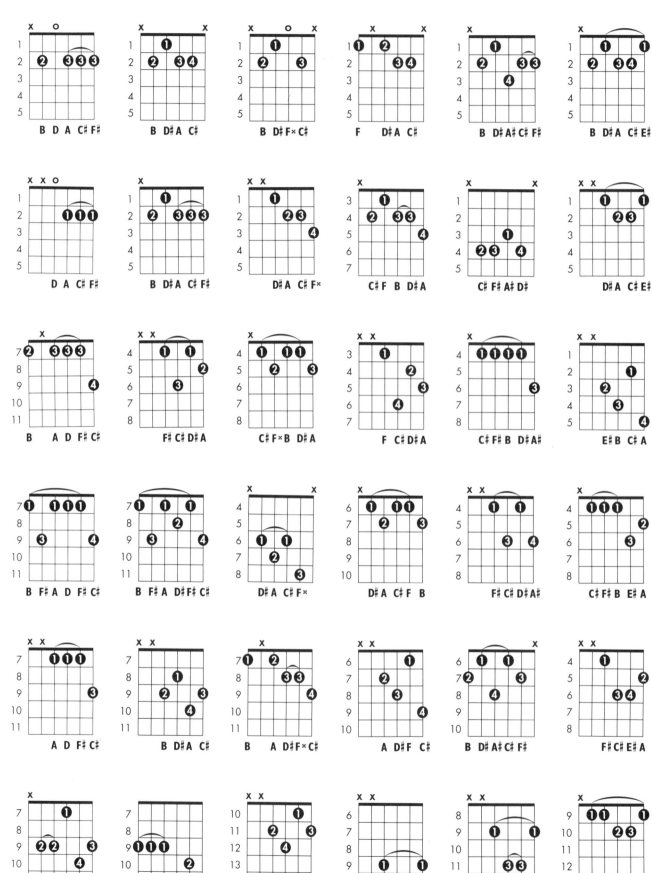

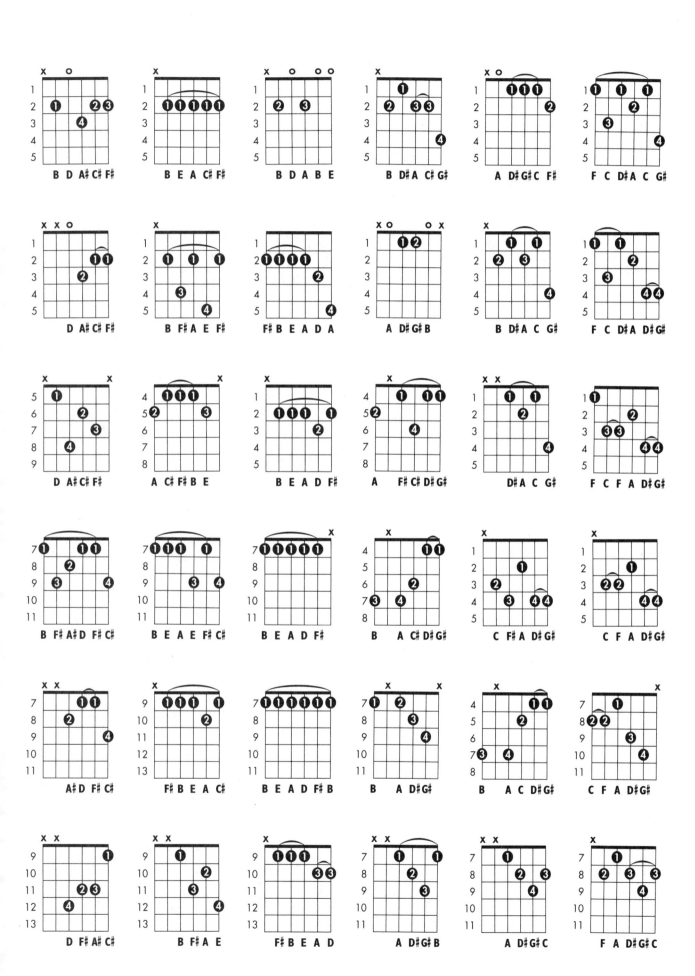

Bm9(maj7)   B11   Bm11   B13   B13(♭9)   B13(♭9♭5)

B

C	Csus	C(♭5)	C(add9)	C5	Cm

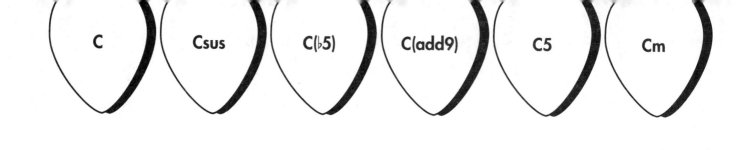

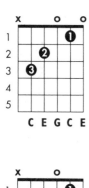 **C**

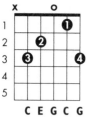 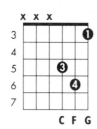 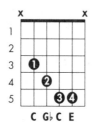 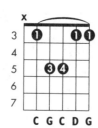 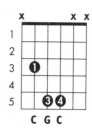 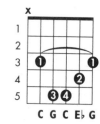

CEGCE · CFGC · G♭CEG♭ · CEGDE · CGC · CE♭GC

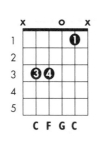 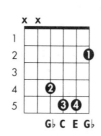 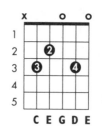 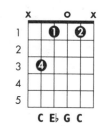

CEGCG · CFG · CG♭CE · CGCDG · CG · CGCE♭G

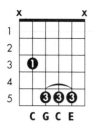 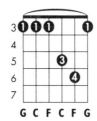 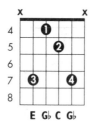 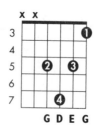 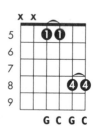 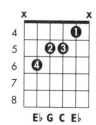

CGCE · GCFCFG · EG♭CG♭ · GDEG · GCGC · E♭GCE♭

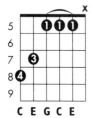 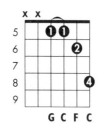 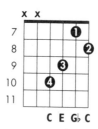 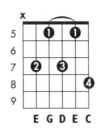 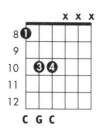 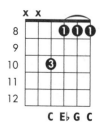

CEGCE · GCFC · CEG♭C · EGDEC · CGC · CE♭GC

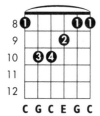 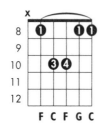 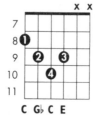 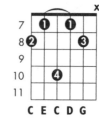 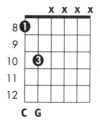 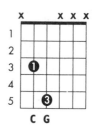

CGCEGC · FCFGC · CG♭CE · CECDG · CG · E♭GCGC

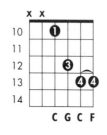 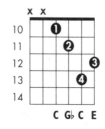 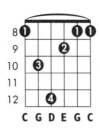 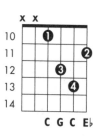

E CGC · CGCF · CG♭CE · CGDEGC · GCGC · CGCE♭

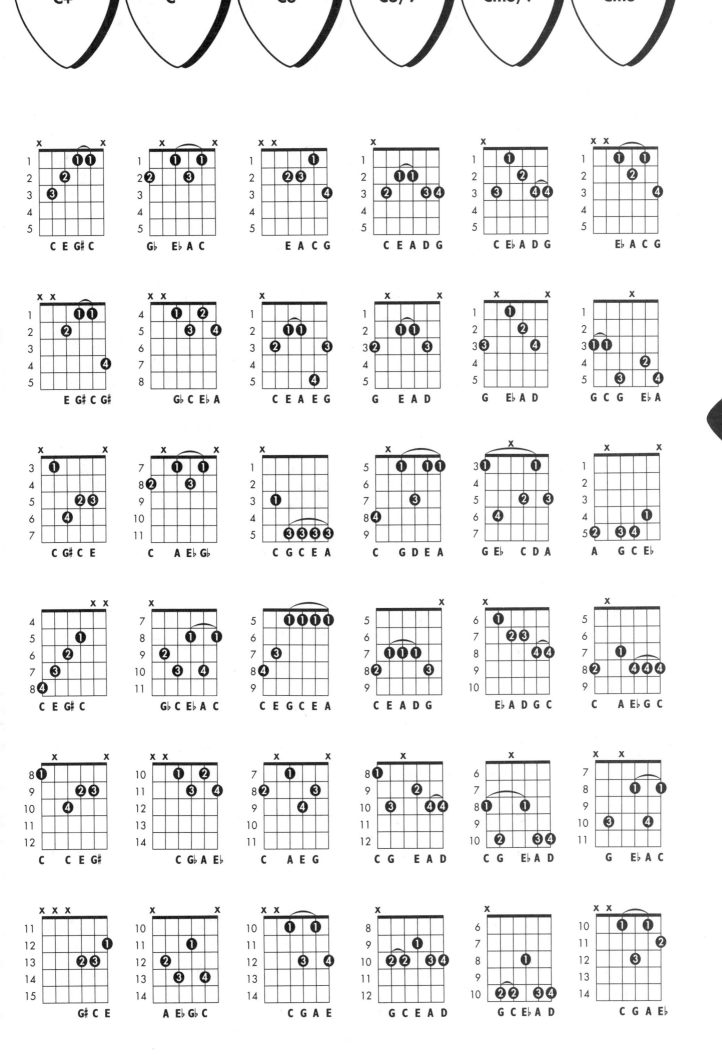

C+   C°   C6   C6/9   Cm6/9   Cm6

C

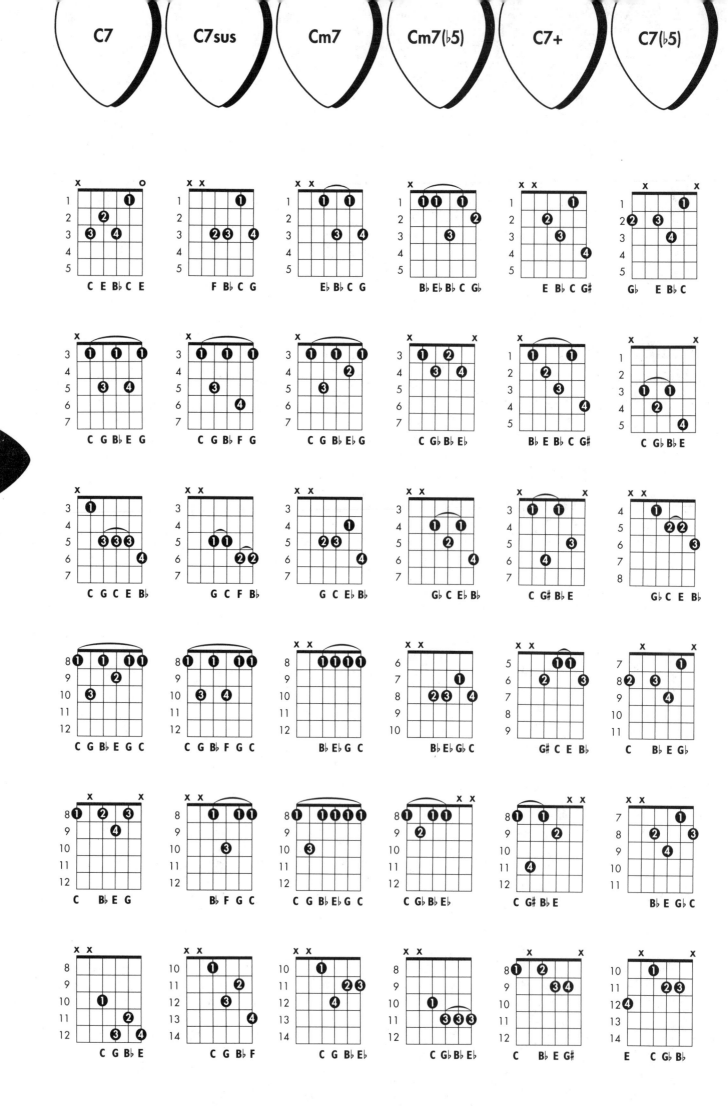

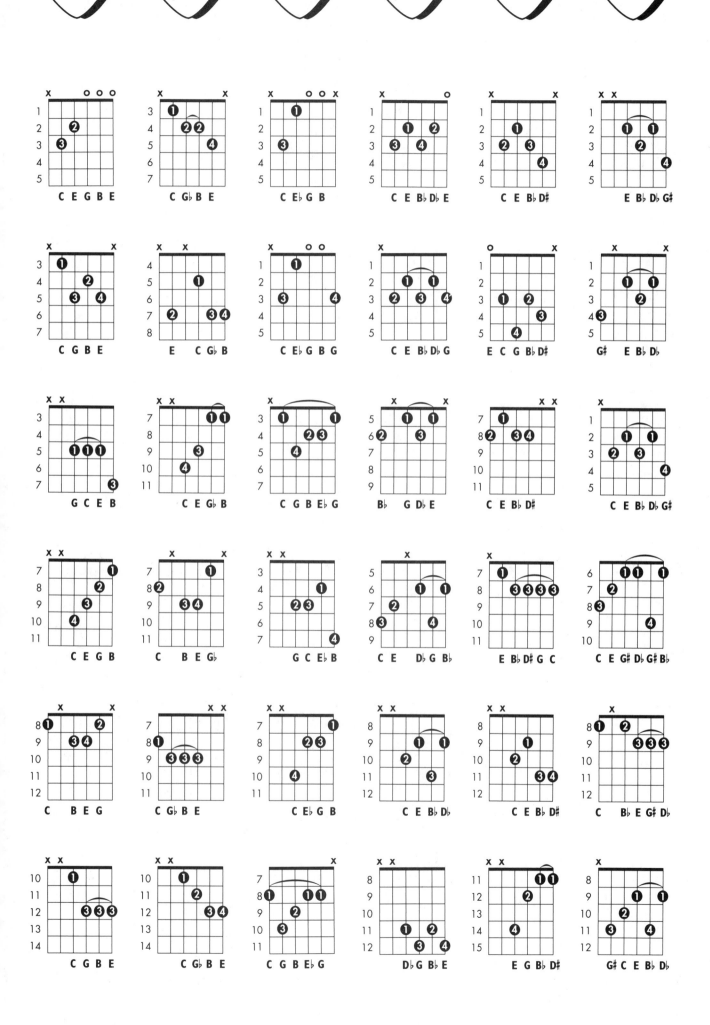

Cmaj7   Cmaj7(♭5)   Cm(maj7)   C7(♭9)   C7(#9)   C7+(♭9)

C

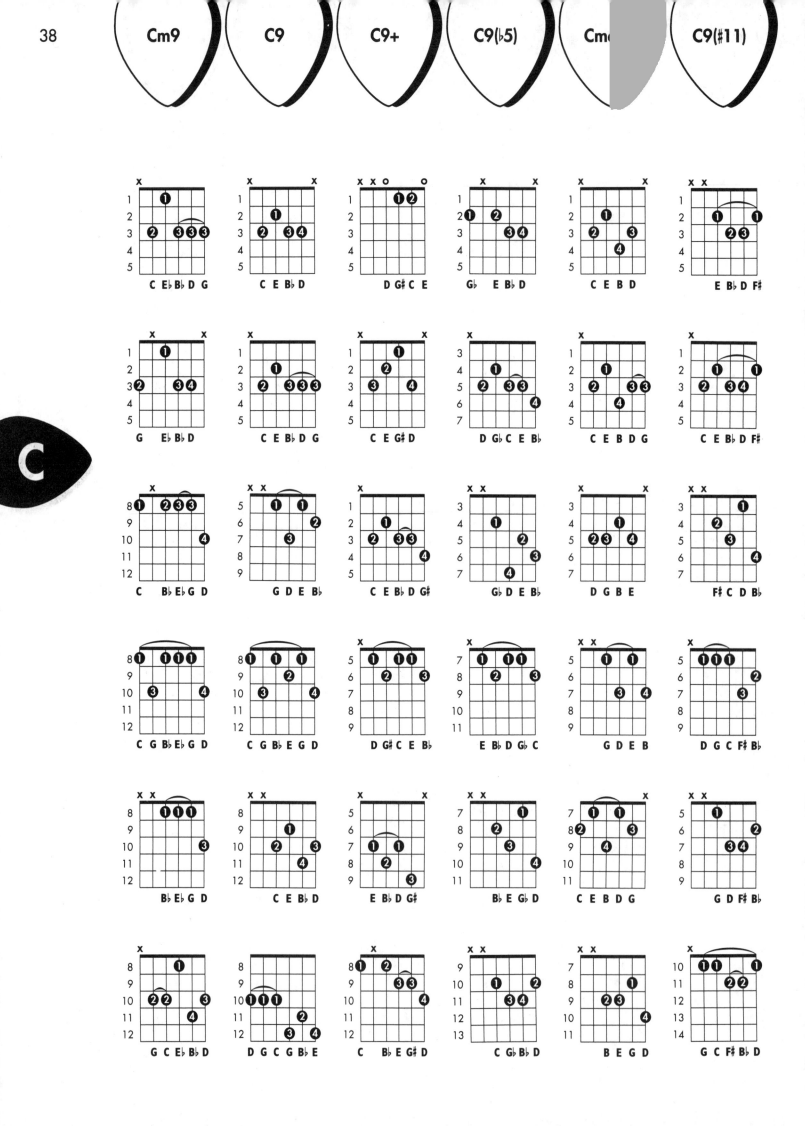

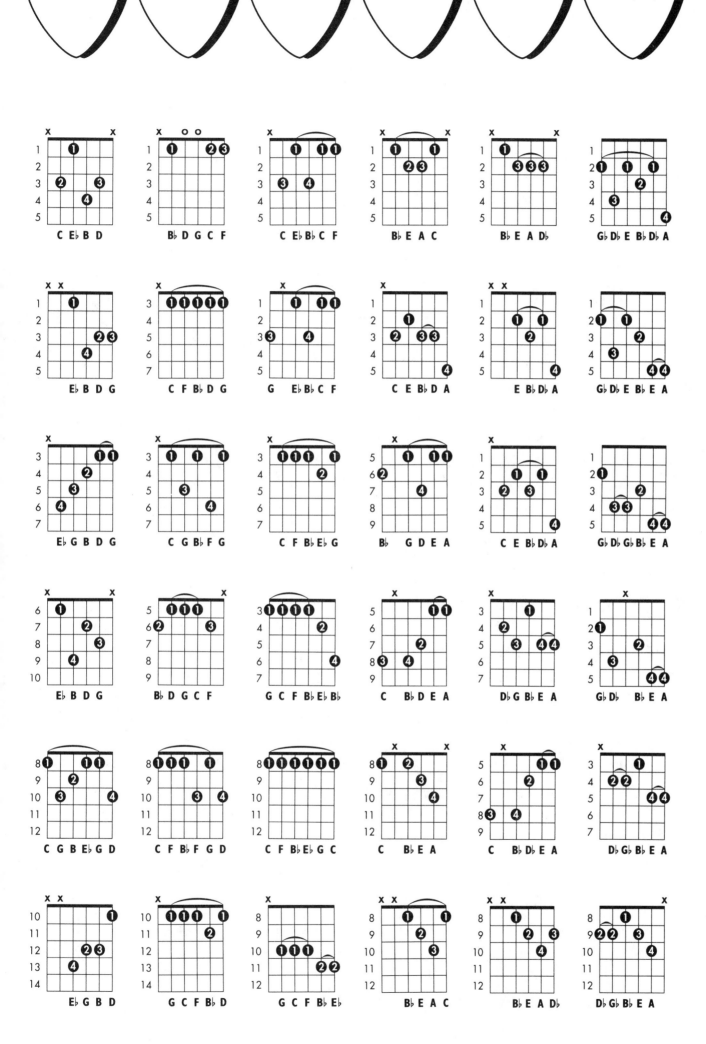

Db

Db	Dbsus	Db(b5)	Db(add9)	Db5	Dbm

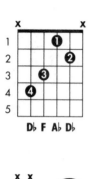 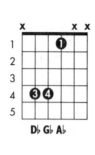 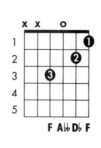 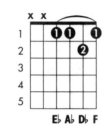 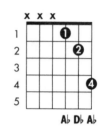 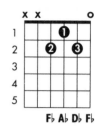

Db F Ab Db | Db Gb Ab | F Abb Db F | Eb Ab Db F | Ab Db Ab | Fb Ab Db Fb

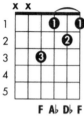 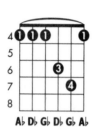 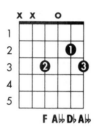 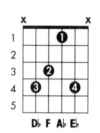 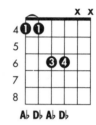 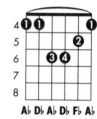

F Ab Db F | Ab Db Gb Db Gb Ab | F Abb Db Ab | Db F Ab Eb | Ab Db Ab Db | Ab Db Ab Db Fb Ab

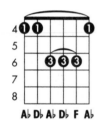 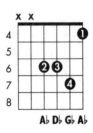 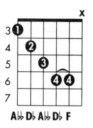 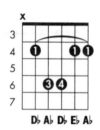 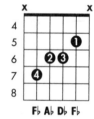 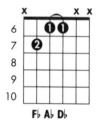

Ab Db Ab Db F Ab | Ab Db Gb Ab | Abb Db Abb Db F | Db Ab Db Eb Ab | Ab Db Ab Db Ab | Fb Ab Db Fb

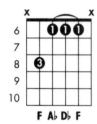 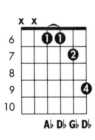 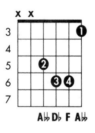 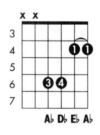 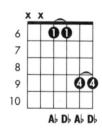 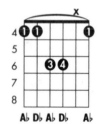

F Ab Db F | Ab Db Gb Db | Abb Db F Abb | Ab Db Eb Ab | Ab Db Ab Db | Fb Ab Db

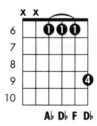 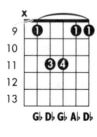 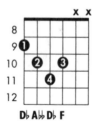 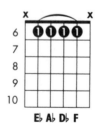 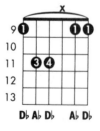 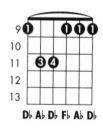

F Ab Db F | Ab Db Gb Db | Db Abb Db F | Eb Ab Db F | Db Ab Db Ab Db | Fb Ab Db

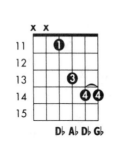 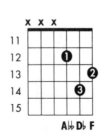 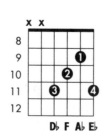 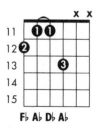

Db Ab Db F Ab Db | Db Ab Db Gb | Abb Db F | Db F Ab Eb | Ab Db Ab Db | Fb Ab Db Ab

Db+ Db° Db6 Db6/9 Dbm6/9 Dbm6

Db

Db+	Db°	Db6	Db6/9	Dbm6/9	Dbm6
F Db F A	Fb Cbb Db Abb	F Bb F Ab Db F	Ab Db F Bb Eb	Ab Db Fb Bb Eb	Fb Bb Fb Ab Db
F A Db F	Abb Db Abb Cbb Fb Abb	F Bb Db Ab	Db F Bb Eb Ab	Ab Fb Bb Eb	Fb Bb Db Ab
A Db F Db	Cbb Fb Abb Db	Ab Db Ab Db F Bb	Db Ab Eb F Bb	Db Fb Bb Eb Ab	Db Ab Bb Fb
A Db F A	Cbb Fb Cbb Db Abb Cbb	F Ab Db F Bb	Db F Bb Eb Ab	Ab Fb Db Eb Bb	Ab Db Fb Bb
Db F A F	Cbb Fb Abb Db	Db Ab Bb F	F Bb Eb Ab Db	Fb Bb Eb Ab Db	Db Ab Db Fb Bb Db
Db F A Db	Db Abb Cbb Fb	Ab Db F Bb	Ab Db F Bb Eb	Ab Db Fb Bb Eb	Fb Bb Db Ab

D♭7   D♭7sus   D♭m7   D♭m7(♭5)   D♭7+   D♭7(♭5)

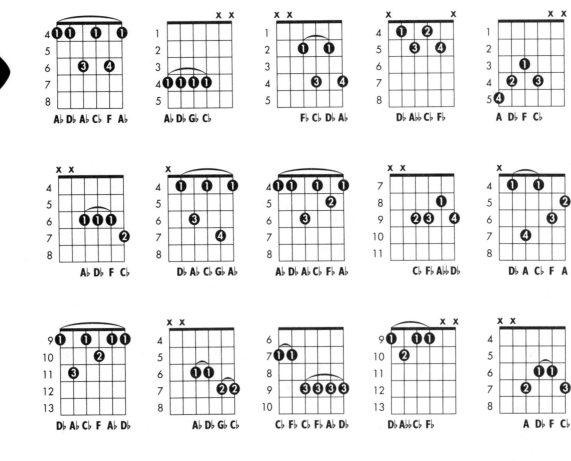

D♭

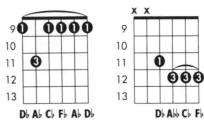
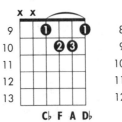
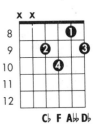

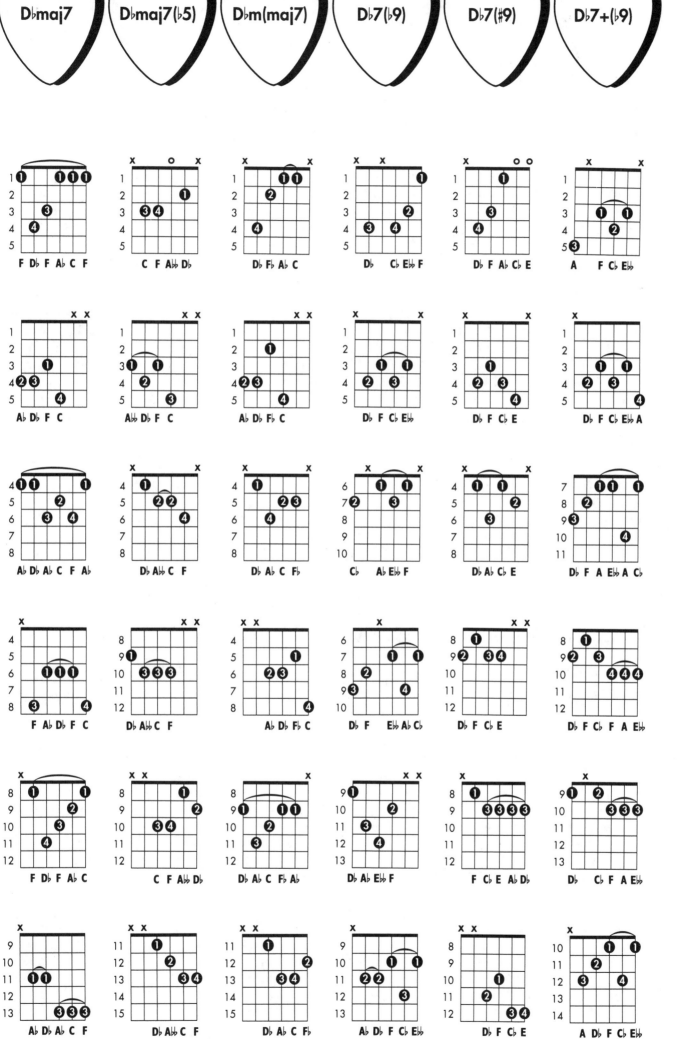

Dbm9	Db9	Db9+	Db9(b5)	Dbmaj9	Db9(#11)

Db

Dbm9	Db9	Db9+	Db9(b5)	Dbmaj9	Db9(#11)
Db Fb Cb Eb	Eb Ab Cb F	F Cb Eb A Db F	Cb Eb Abb Db	F Eb Ab C	Db F Cb Eb G
Fb Cb Eb Ab	F Cb Eb Ab Db F	Db F A Eb	Eb Abb Cb F	Db F C Eb	Ab Db G Cb Eb
Db Fb Cb Eb	Db F Cb Eb	F Cb Eb A	Db F Cb Eb Abb	Db Ab C Eb Ab	G Db Eb Cb
Cb Fb Ab Eb	Eb Ab Db F Cb	Eb A Db F Cb	Db Abb Cb Eb	Eb Ab Db F C	Ab Eb G Cb
Db Fb Cb Eb	F Cb Eb Ab	A Eb F Cb	Db F Cb Eb Abb	C F Ab Eb	F Cb Eb G Db
Fb Db Ab Cb Eb	Cb F Ab Eb	Cb F A Eb	Db Abb Cb Eb	Db Ab C Eb	Ab Db G Cb Eb

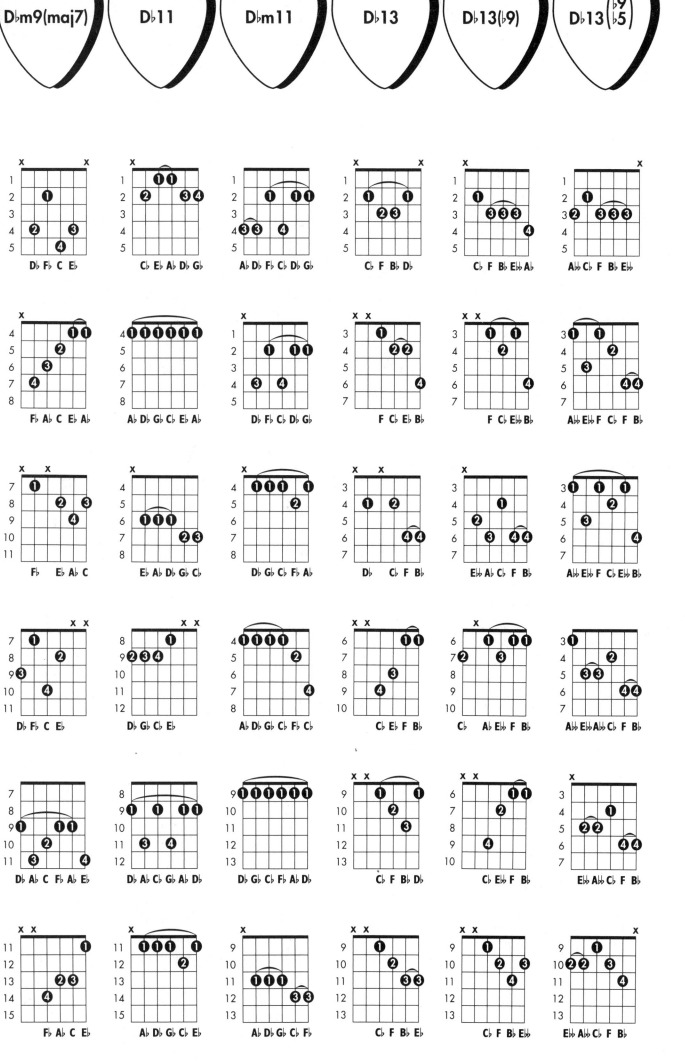

D♭m9(maj7) · D♭11 · D♭m11 · D♭13 · D♭13(♭9) · D♭13($\binom{♭9}{♭5}$)

D♭

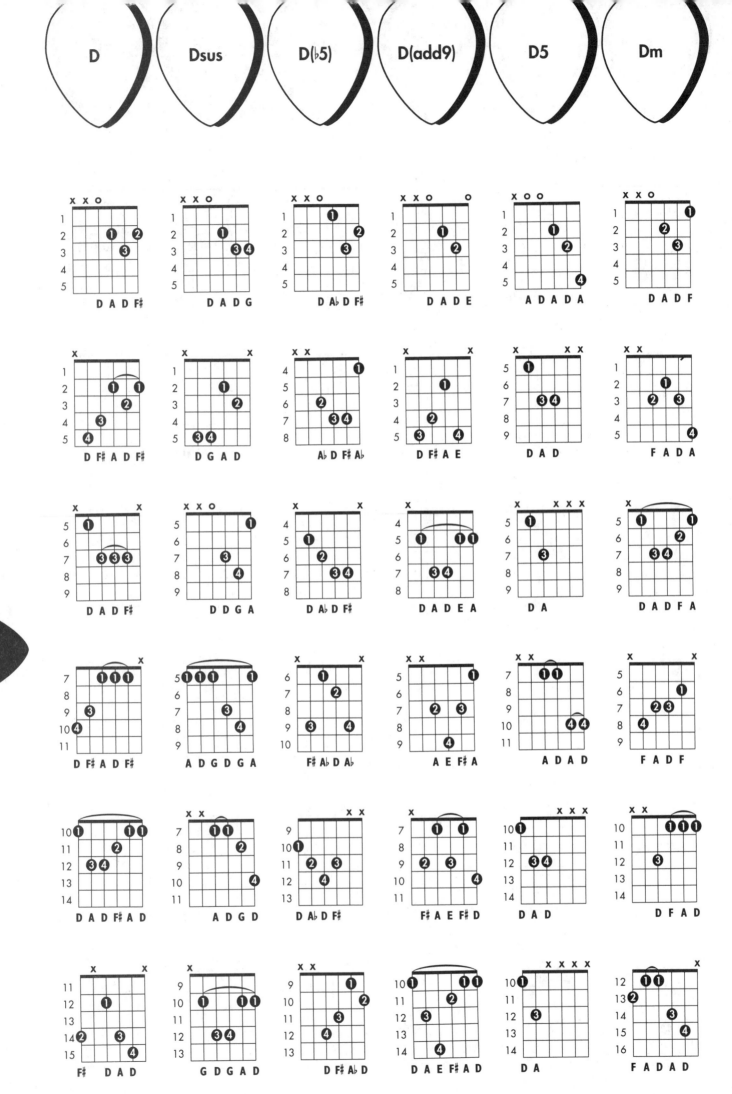

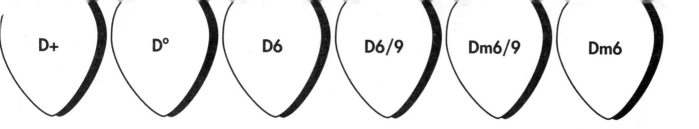

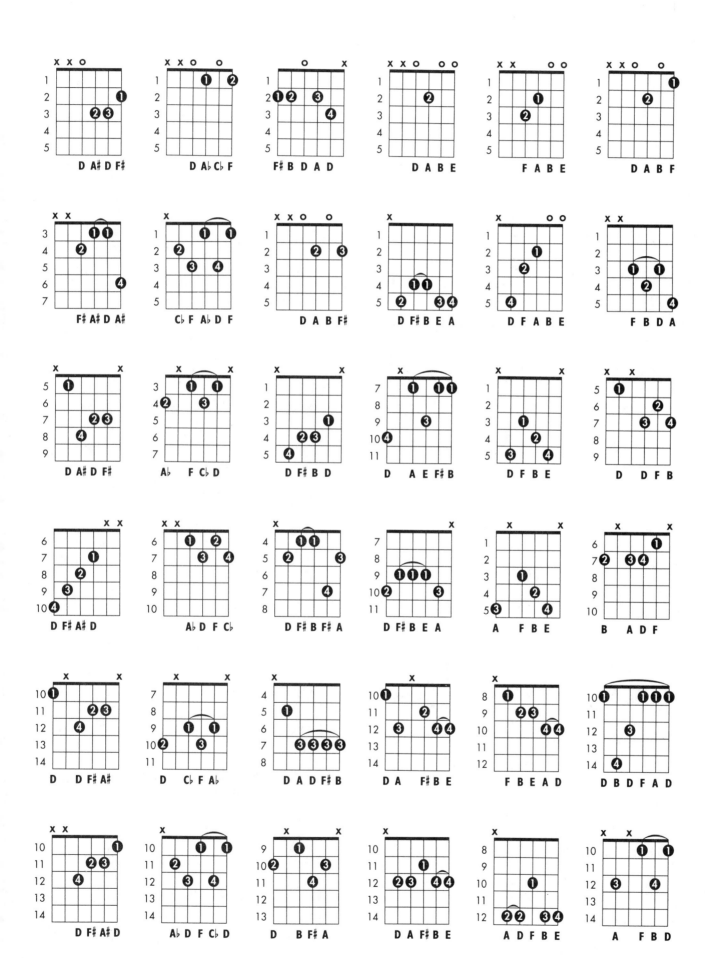

D+ — D A# D F#

D° — D A♭ C♭ F

D6 — F# B D A D

D6/9 — D A B E

Dm6/9 — F A B E

Dm6 — D A B F

F# A# D A#

C♭ F A♭ D F

D A B F#

D F# B E A

D F A B E

F B D A

D A# D F#

A♭ F C♭ D

D F# B D

D A E F# B

D F B E

D D F B

D F# A# D

A♭ D F C♭

D F# B F# A

D F# B E A

A F B E

B A D F

D D F# A#

D C♭ F A♭

D A D F# B

D A F# B E

F B E A D

D B D F A D

D F# A# D

A♭ D F C♭ D

D B F# A

D A F# B E

A D F B E

A F B D

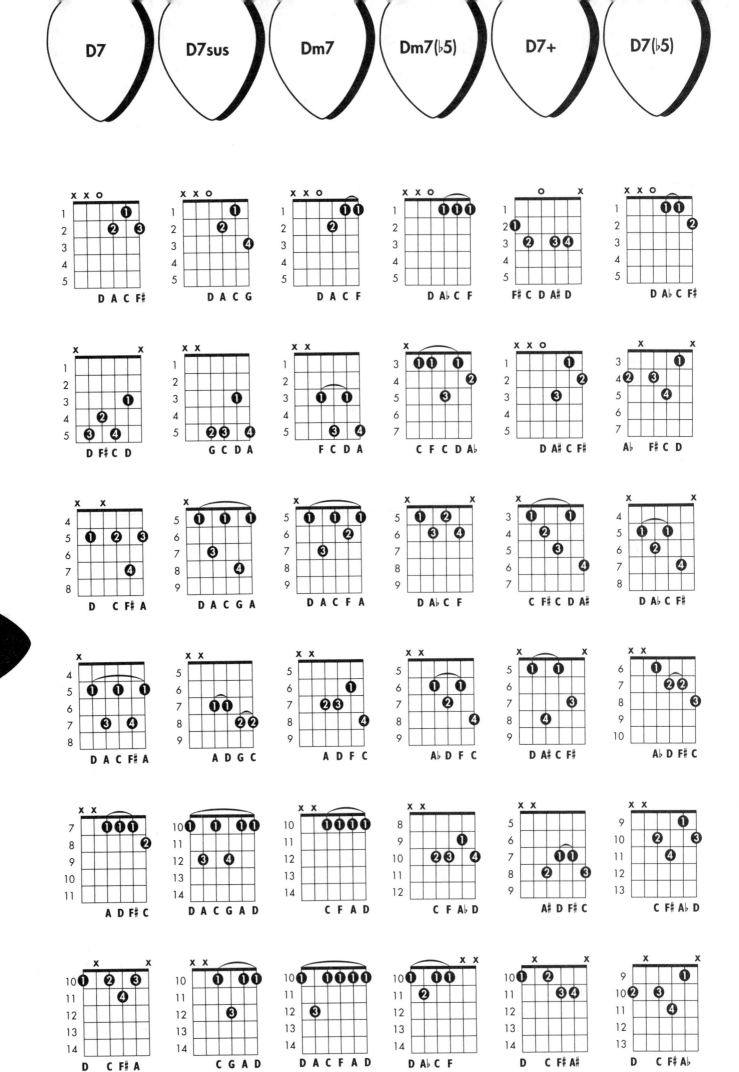

Dmaj7 | Dmaj7(♭5) | Dm(maj7) | D7(♭9) | D7(♯9) | D7+(♭9)

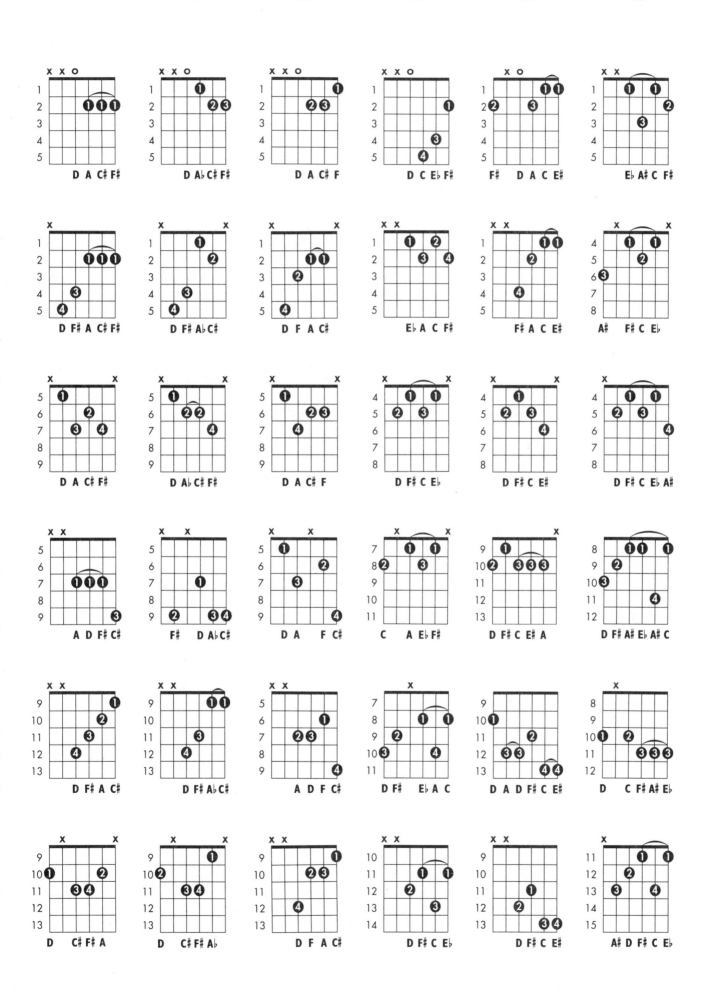

D

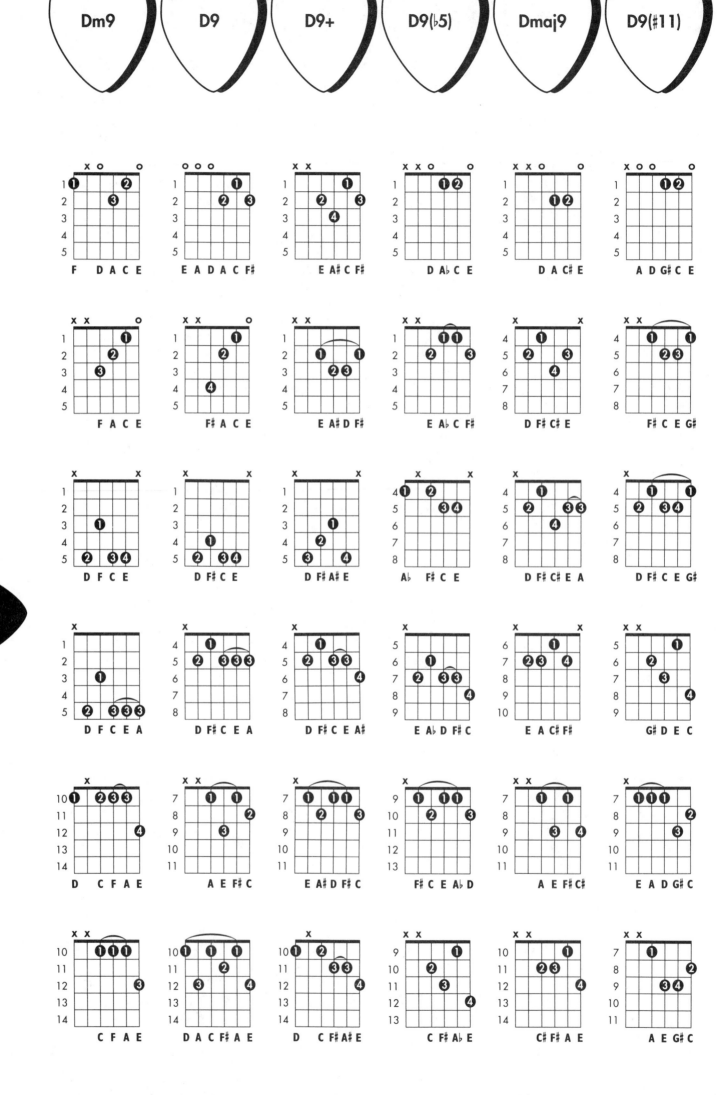

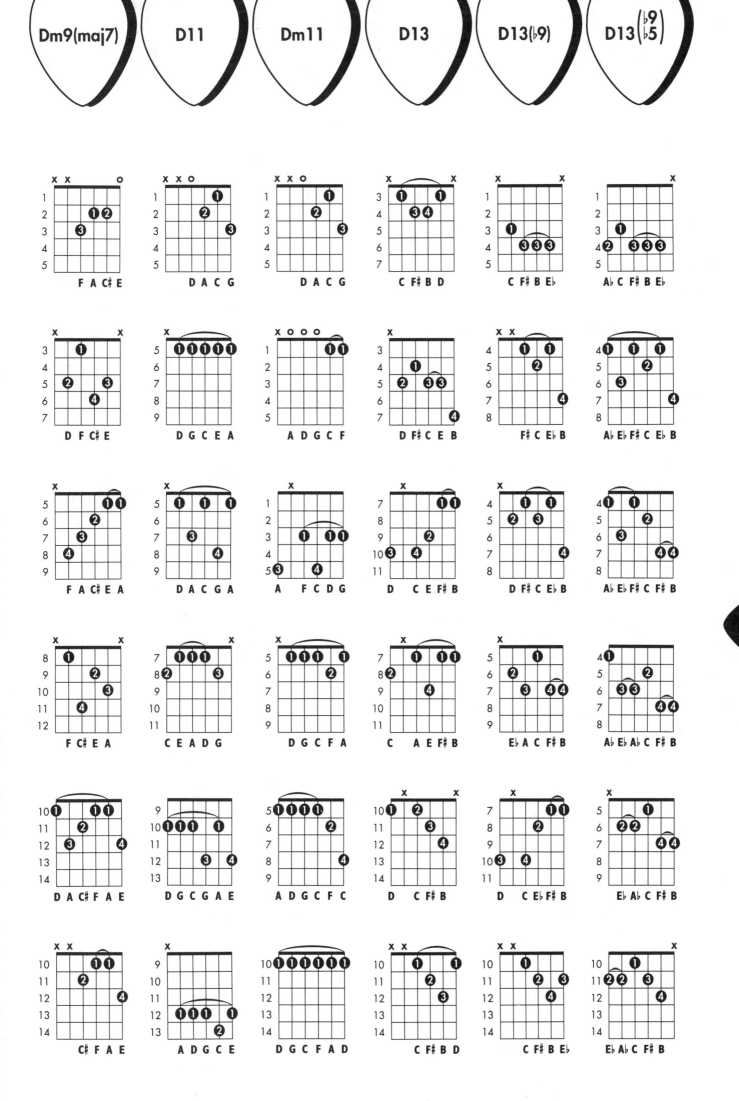

Dm9(maj7)   D11   Dm11   D13   D13(♭9)   D13(♭9 ♭5)

D

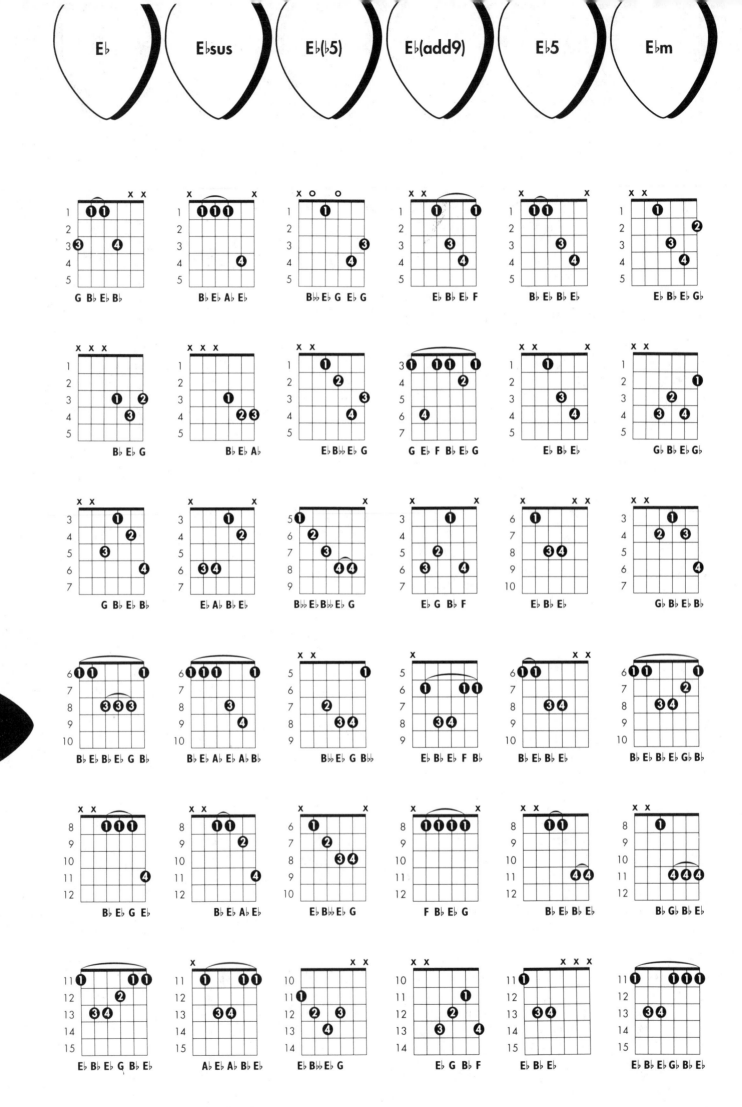

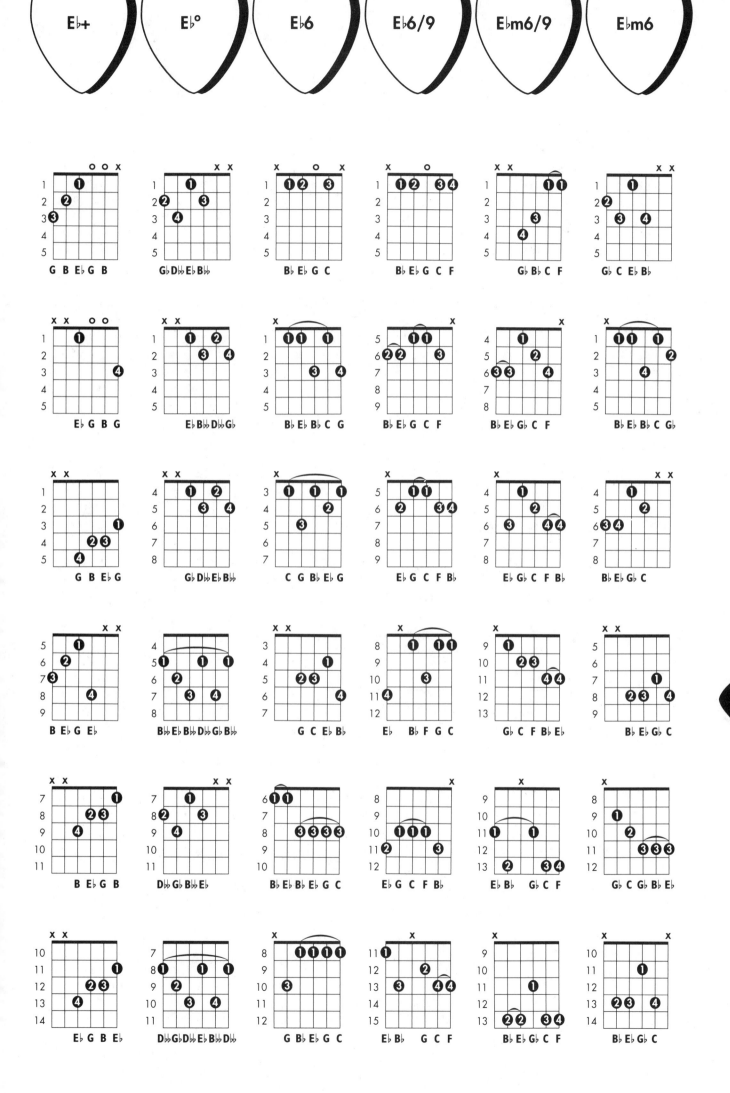

E♭7 **E♭7sus** **E♭m7** **E♭m7(♭5)** **E♭7+** **E♭7(♭5)**

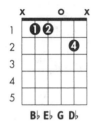 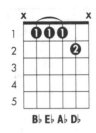 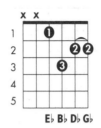 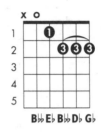 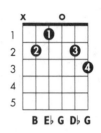 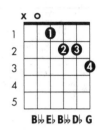

B♭ E♭ G D♭ | B♭ E♭ A♭ D♭ | E♭ B♭ D♭ G♭ | B♭♭ E♭ B♭♭ D♭ G♭ | B E♭ G D♭ G | B♭♭ E♭ B♭♭ D♭ G

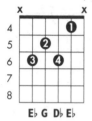 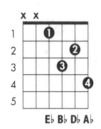 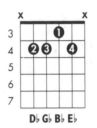 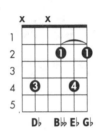 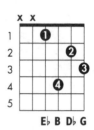 

E♭ G D♭ E♭ | E♭ B♭ D♭ A♭ | D♭ G♭ B♭ E♭ | D♭ B♭♭ E♭ G♭ | E♭ B D♭ G | G D♭ E♭ B♭♭

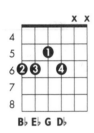 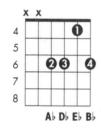 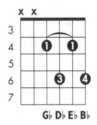 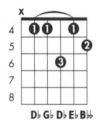 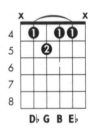 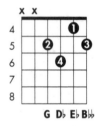

B♭ E♭ G D♭ | A♭ D♭ E♭ B♭ | G♭ D♭ E♭ B♭ | D♭ G♭ D♭ E♭ B♭ | D♭ G B E♭ | G D♭ E♭ B♭♭

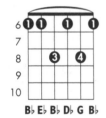 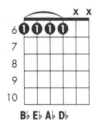 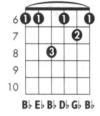 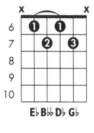 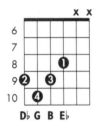 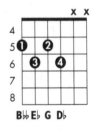

B♭ E♭ B♭ D♭ G B♭ | B♭ E♭ A♭ D♭ | B♭ E♭ B♭ D♭ G♭ B♭ | E♭ B♭♭ D♭ G♭ | D♭ G B E♭ | B♭♭ E♭ G D♭

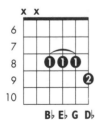 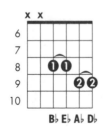 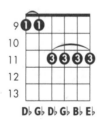 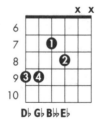 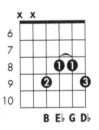 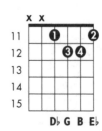

B♭ E♭ G D♭ | B♭ E♭ A♭ D♭ | D♭ G♭ D♭ G♭ B♭ E♭ | D♭ G♭ B♭♭ E♭ | B E♭ G D♭ | B♭♭ E♭ G D♭

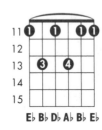 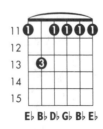 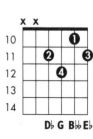

E♭ B♭ D♭ G B♭ E♭ | E♭ B♭ D♭ A♭ B♭ E♭ | E♭ B♭ D♭ G♭ B♭ E♭ | E♭ B♭♭ D♭ G♭ | D♭ G B E♭ | D♭ G B♭♭ E♭

E♭

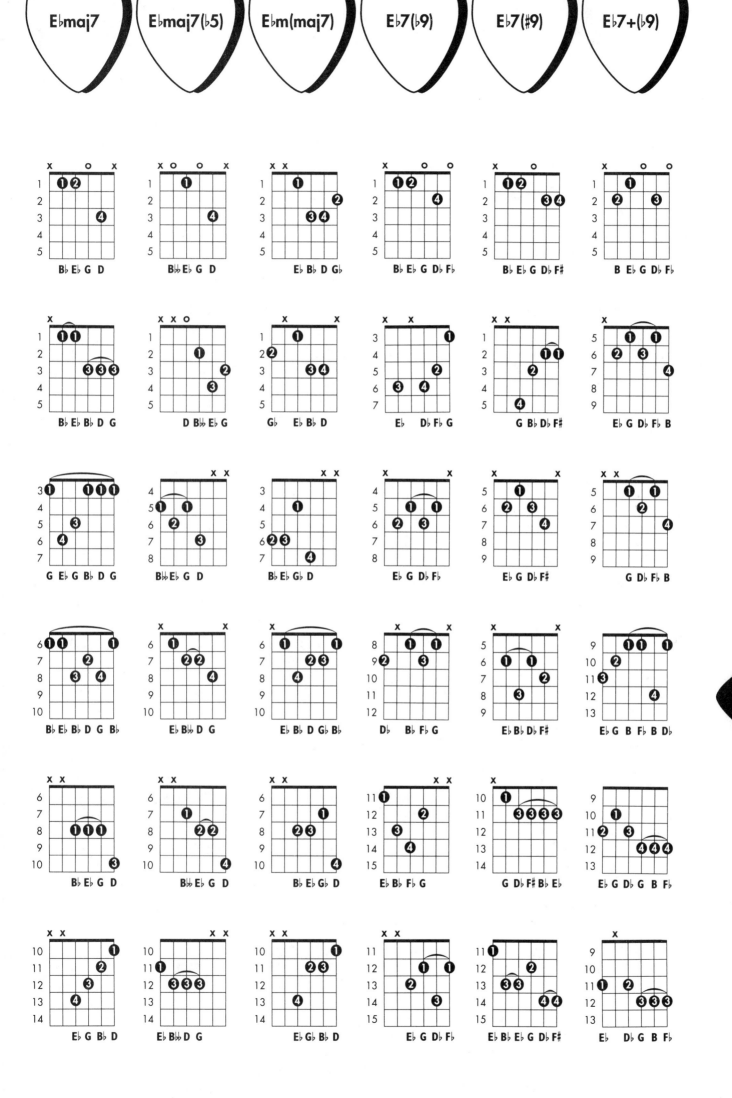

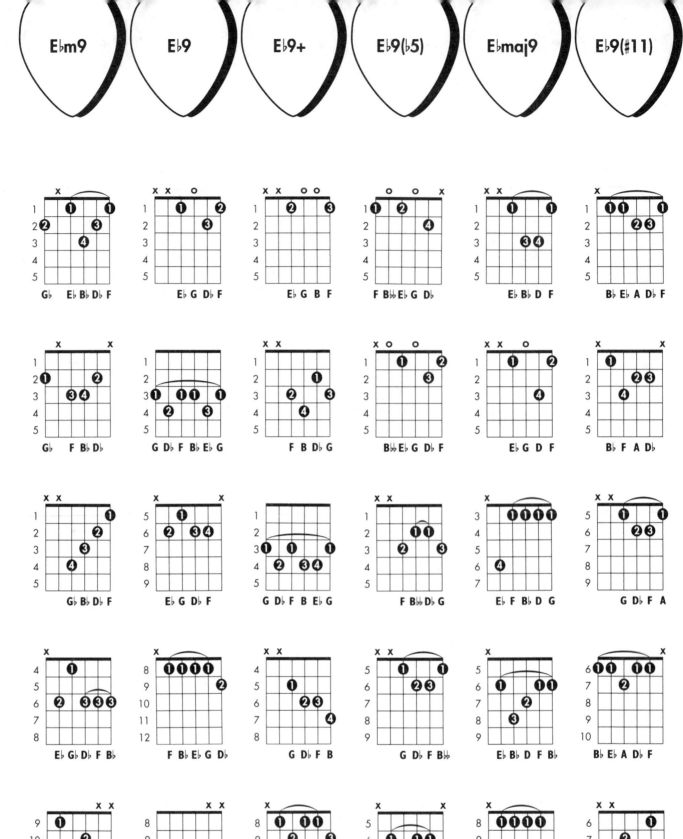

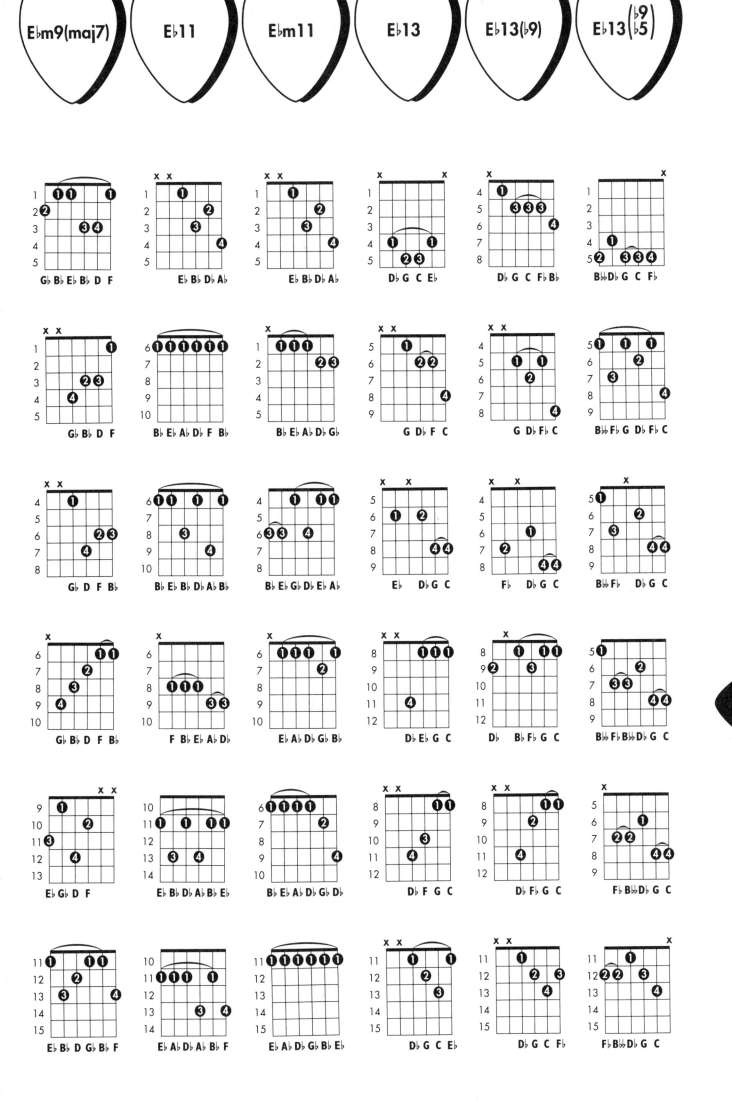

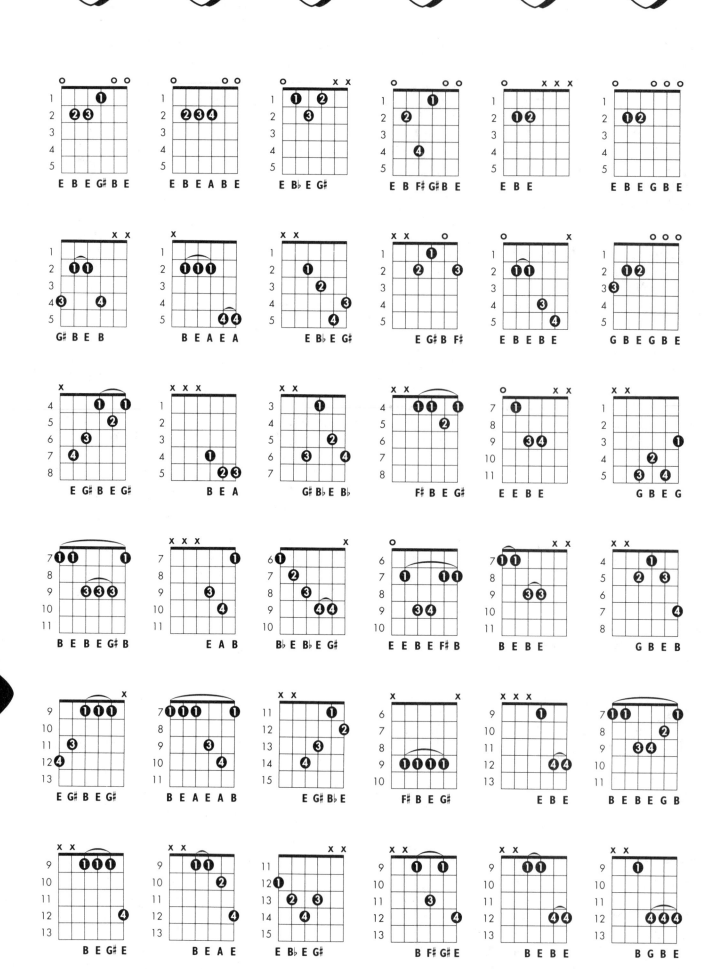

E   Esus   E(♭5)   E(add9)   E5   Em

E

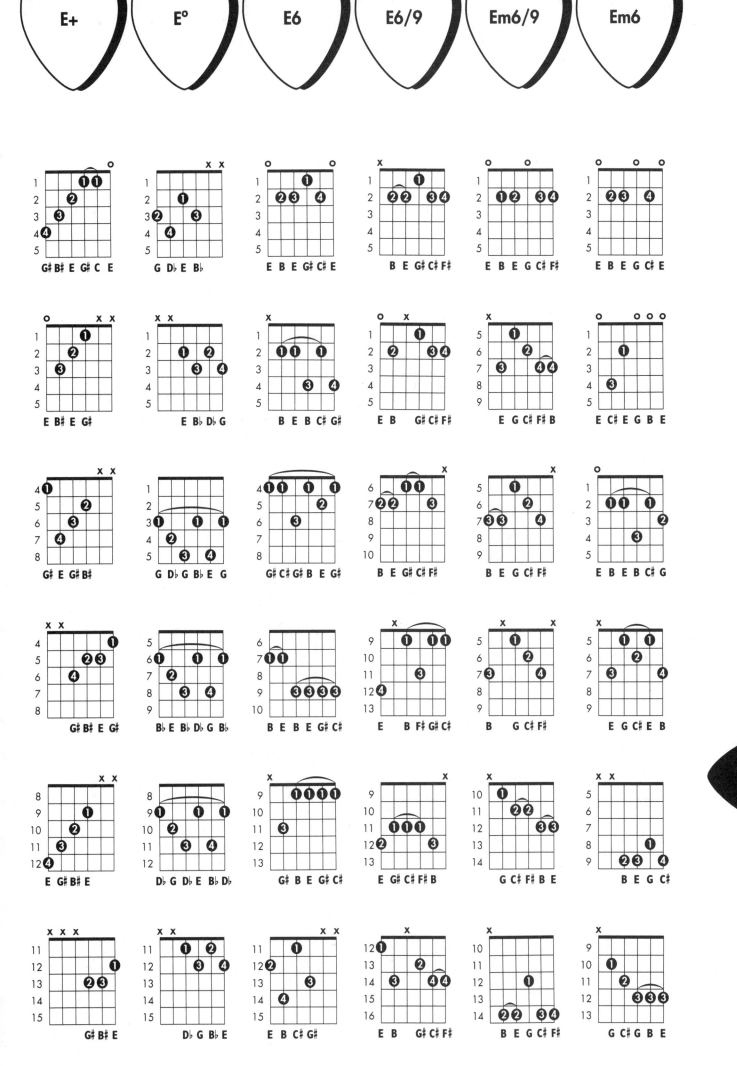

E+   E°   E6   E6/9   Em6/9   Em6

E

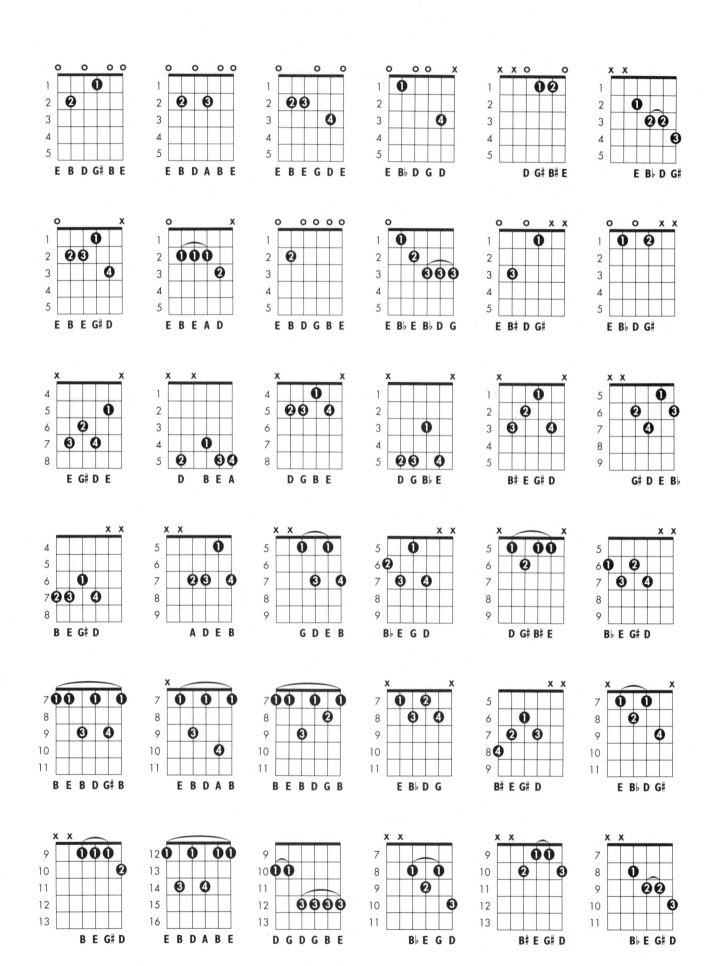

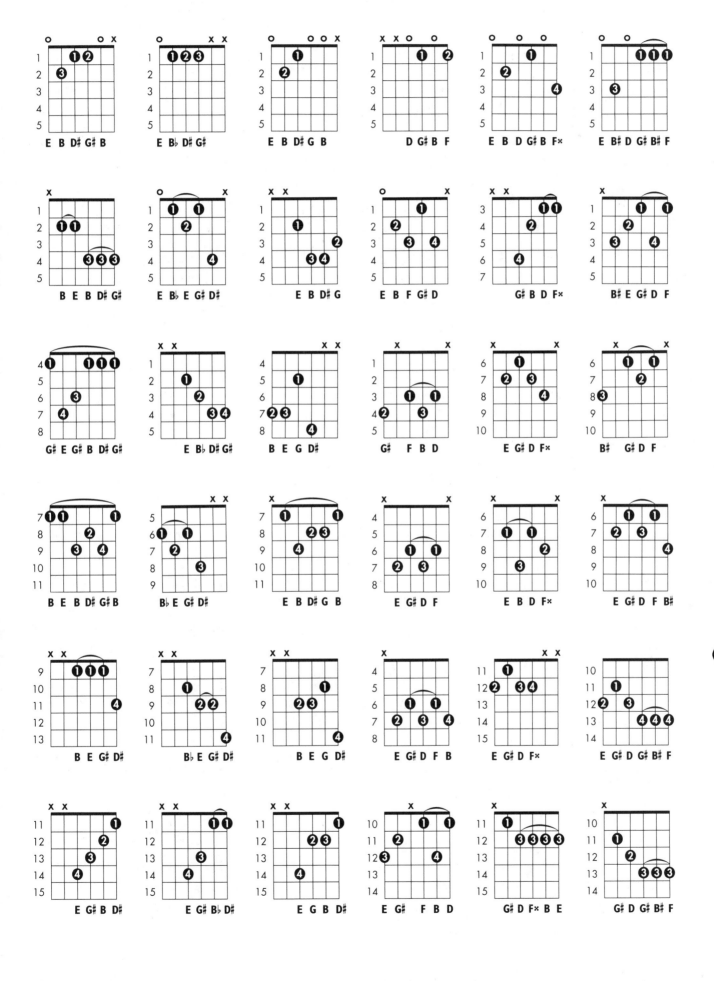

Em9	E9	E9+	E9(♭5)	Emaj9	E9(#11)
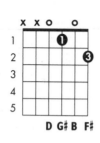	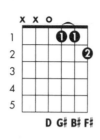	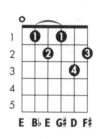	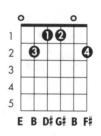	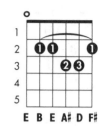	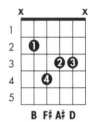
D G B F#	D G# B F#	D G# B# F#	E B♭ E G# D F#	E B D# G# B F#	E B E A# D F#
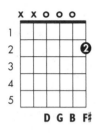	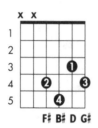	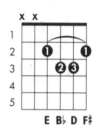	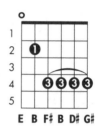	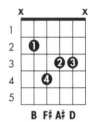	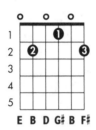
E B D G B F#	E B D G# B F#	F# B# D G#	E B♭ D F#	E B F# B D# G#	B F# A# D
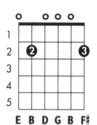	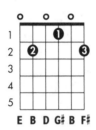	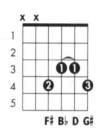	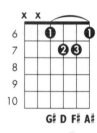	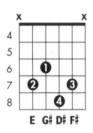	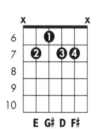
E B E G D F#	E G# D F#	G# D F# B# E G#	F# B♭ D G#	E G# D# F#	G# D F# A#
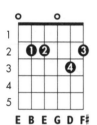	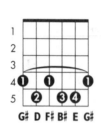	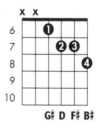	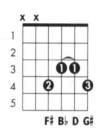	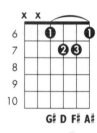	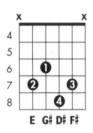
E G D F#	G# D F# B	G# D F# B#	E G# D F# B♭	E B D# F# B	B E A# D F#
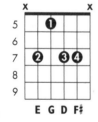	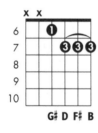	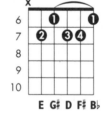	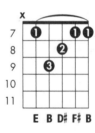	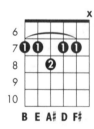	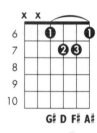
G D F# B	F# B E G# D	B# F# G# D	E B♭ D F#	F# B E G# D	A# E F# D
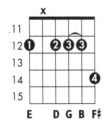	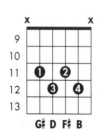	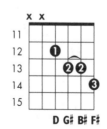	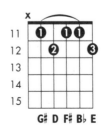	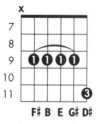	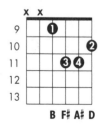
E D G B F#	G# D F# B	D G# B# F#	G# D F# B♭ E	G# D# F# B	B F# A# D

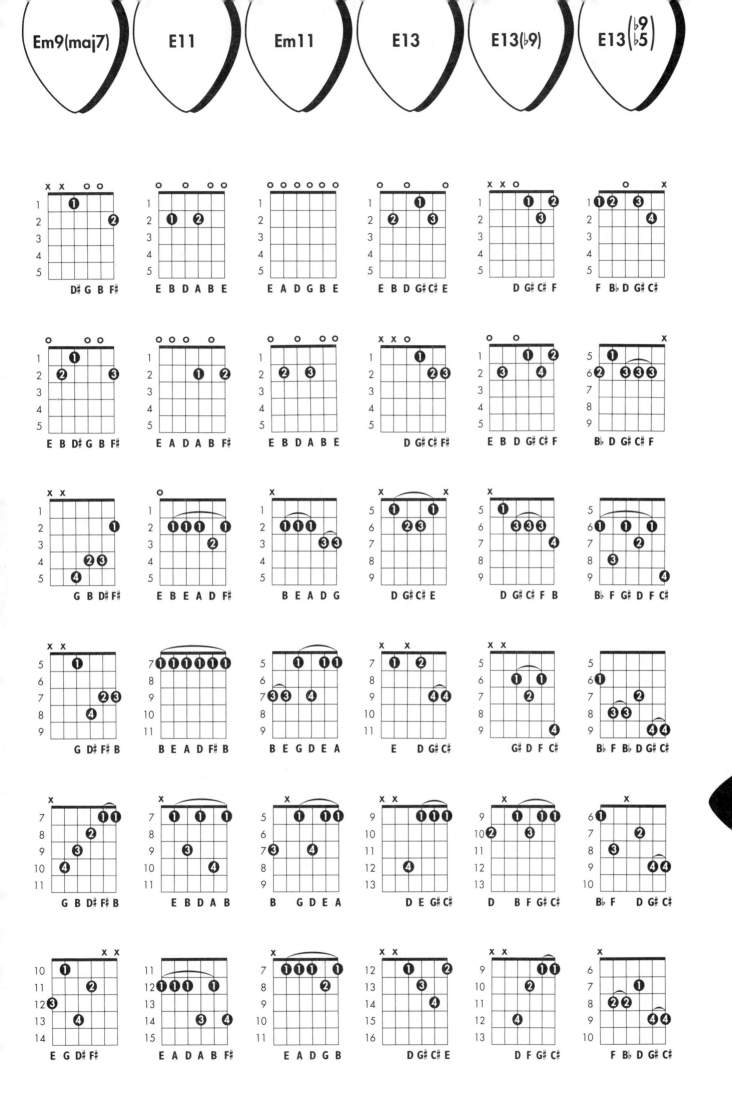

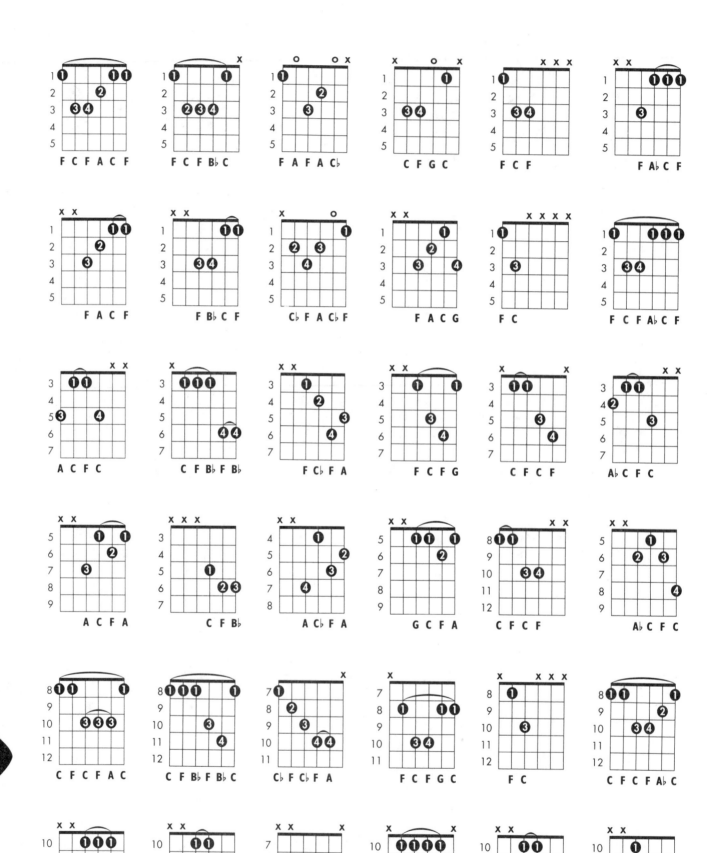

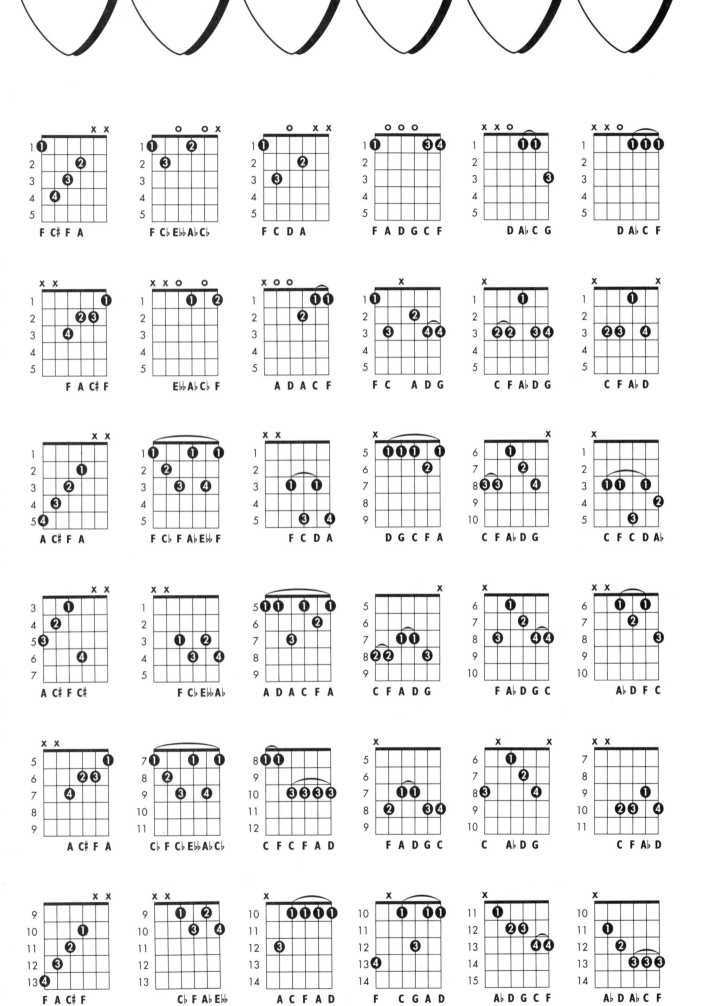

F+   F°   F6   F6/9   Fm6/9   Fm6

F

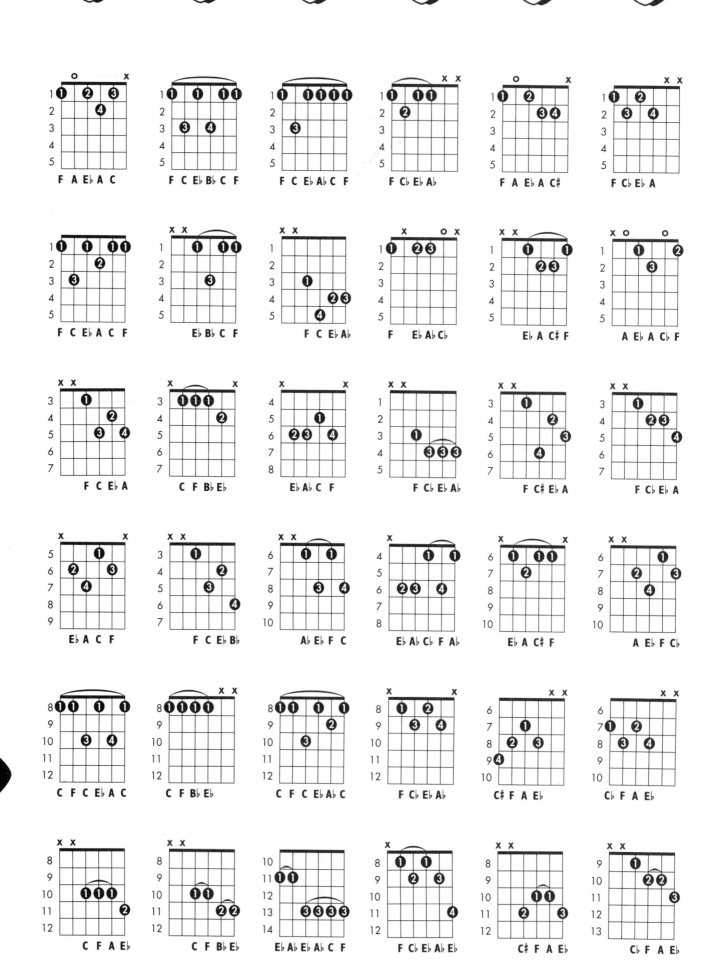

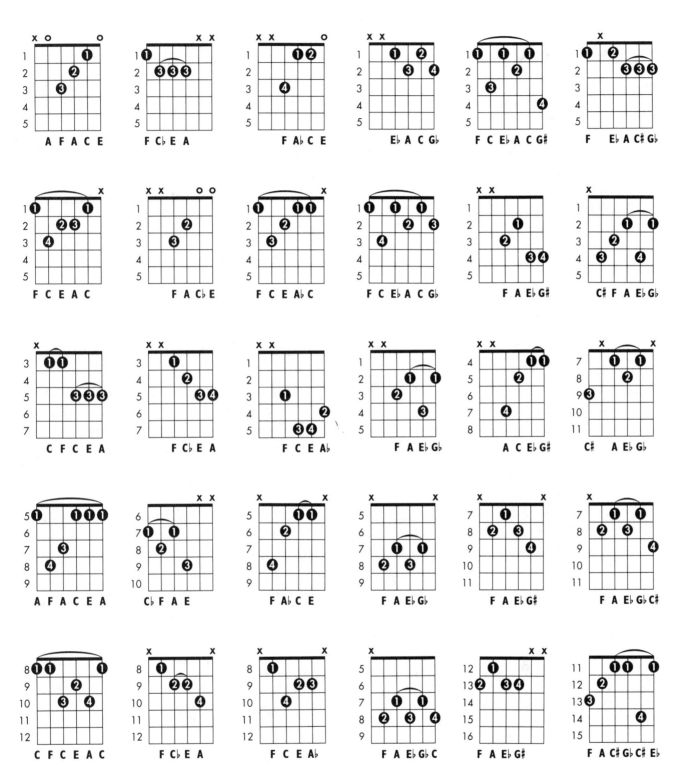

| Fmaj7 | Fmaj7(♭5) | Fm(maj7) | F7(♭9) | F7(♯9) | F7+(♭9) |

F

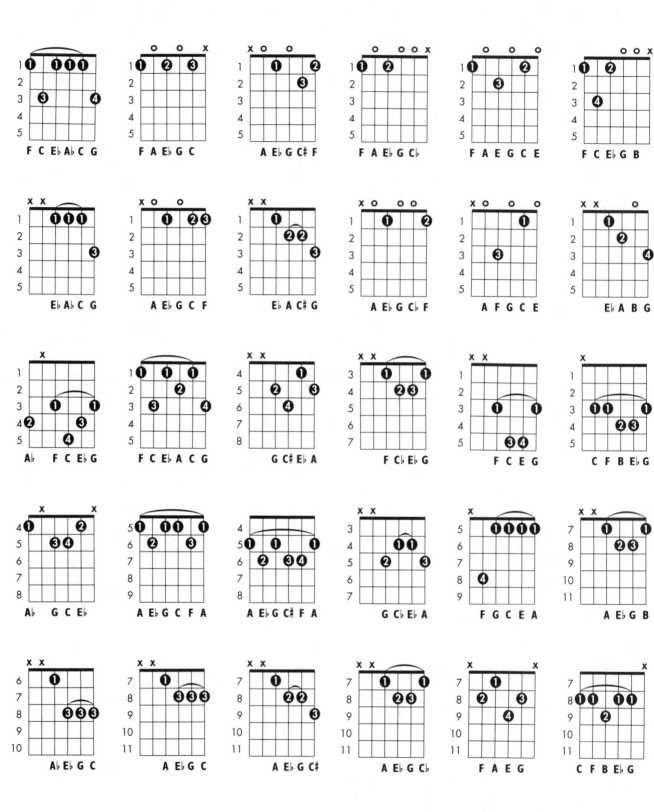

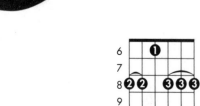

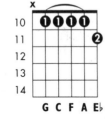

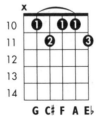

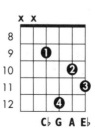

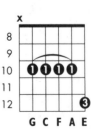

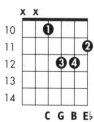

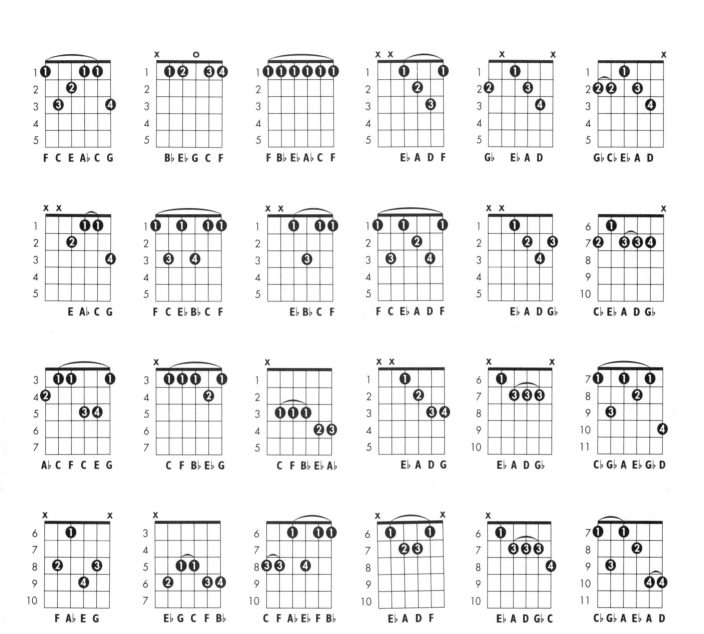

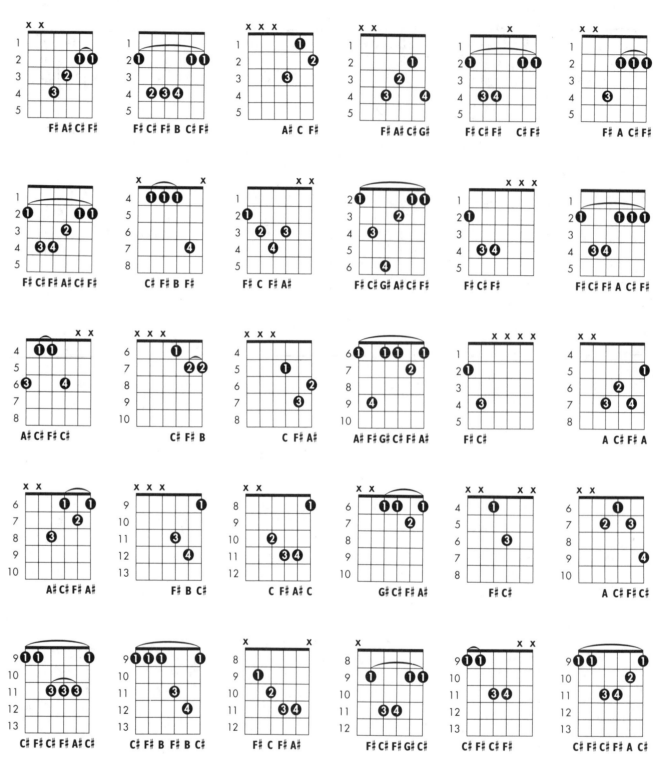

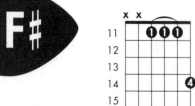

F#+	F#°	F#6	F#6/9	F#m6/9	F#m6

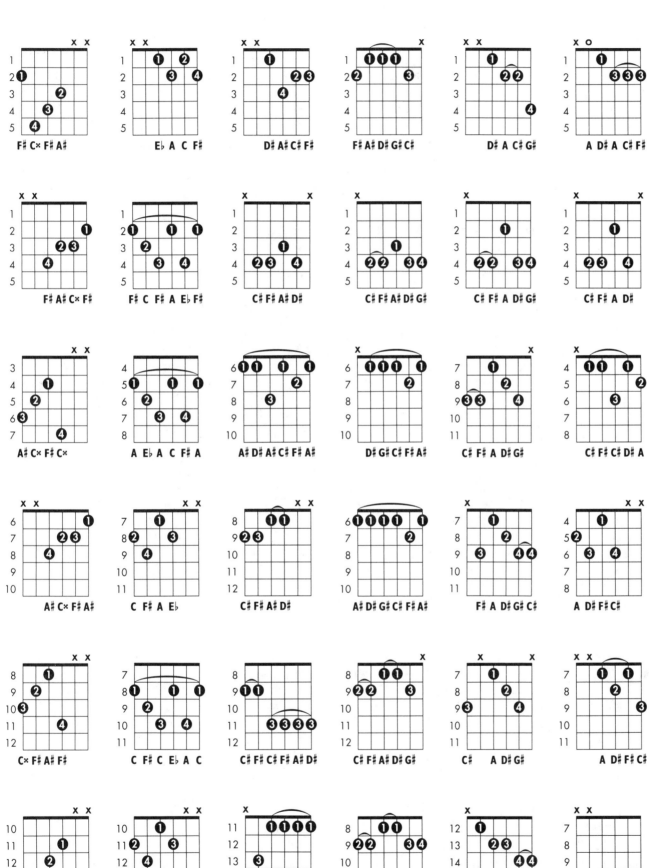

F# C× F# A# | E♭ A C F# | D# A# C# F# | F# A# D# G# C# | D# A C# G# | A D# A C# F#

F# A# C× F# | F# C F# A E♭ F# | C# F# A# D# | C# F# A# D# G# | C# F# A D# G# | C# F# A D#

A# C× F# C× | A E♭ A C F# A | A# D# A# C# F# A# | D# G# C# F# A | C# F# A D# G# | C# F# C# D# A

A# C× F# A# | C F# A E♭ | C# F# A# D# | A# D# G# C# F# A | F# A D# G# C# | A D# F# C#

C× F# A# F# | C F# C E♭ A C | C# F# C# F# A# D# | C# F# A# D# G# | C# A D# G# | A D# F# C#

F# A# C× F# | E♭ A C F# | A# C# F# A# D# | C# F# A# D# G# C# | A D# G# C# F# | C# F# A D#

F#

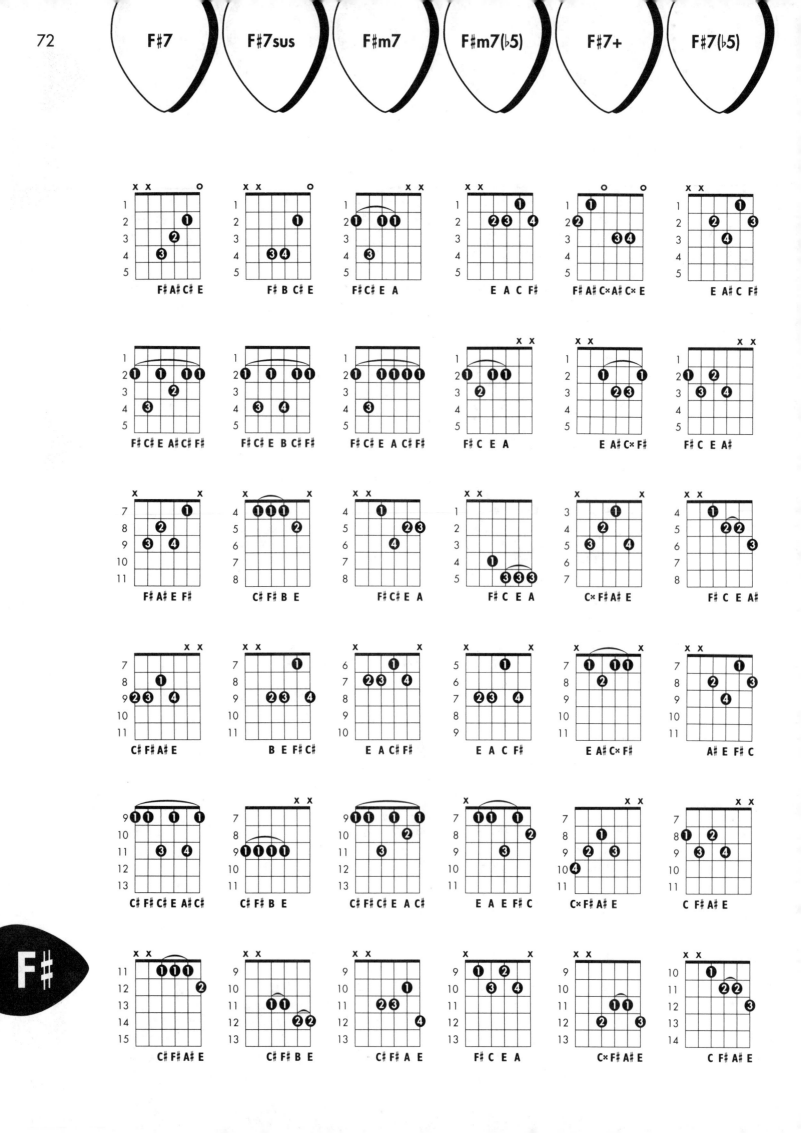

F#7 | F#7sus | F#m7 | F#m7(♭5) | F#7+ | F#7(♭5)

F#maj7 F#maj7(♭5) F#m(maj7) F#7(♭9) F#7(#9) F#7+(♭9)

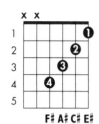 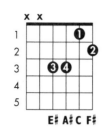 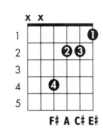 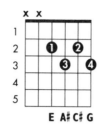 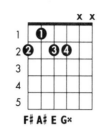 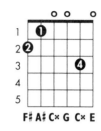

F# A# C# E#   E# A# C F#   F# A C# E#   E A# C# G   F# A# E G×   F# A# C× G C× E

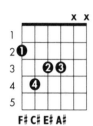 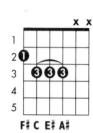 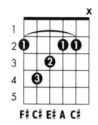 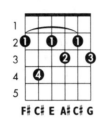 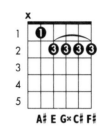 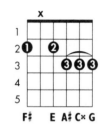

F# C# E# A#   F# C E# A#   F# C# E# A C#   F# C# E A# C# G   A# E G× C# F#   F# E A# C× G

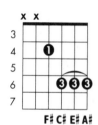 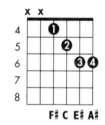 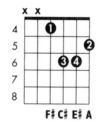 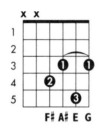 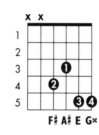 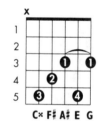

F# C# E# A#   F# C E# A#   F# C# E# A   F# A# E G   F# A# E G×   C× F# A# E G

 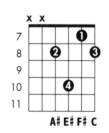 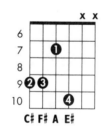 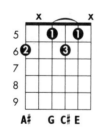 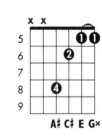 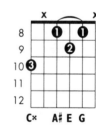

A# F# A# C# E# A#   A# E# F# C   C# F# A E#   A# G C# E   A# C# E G×   C× A# E G

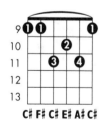 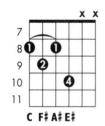 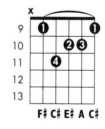 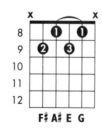 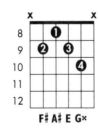 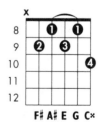

C# F# C# E# A# C#   C F# A# E#   F# C# E# A C#   F# A# E G   F# A# E G×   F# A# E G C×

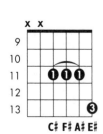 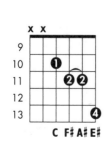 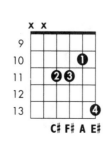 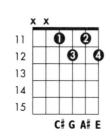 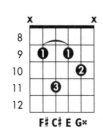 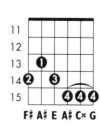

C# F# A# E#   C F# A E#   C# F# A E#   C# G A# E   F# C# E G×   F# A# E A# C× G

F#

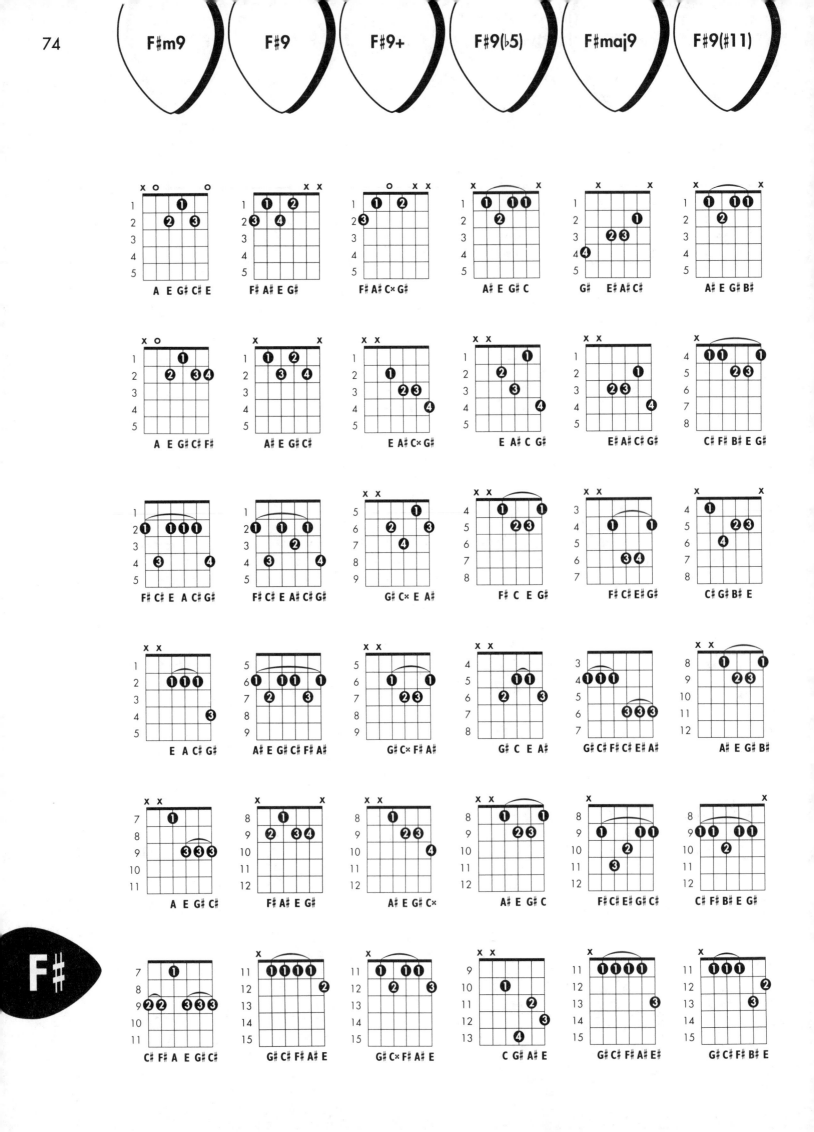

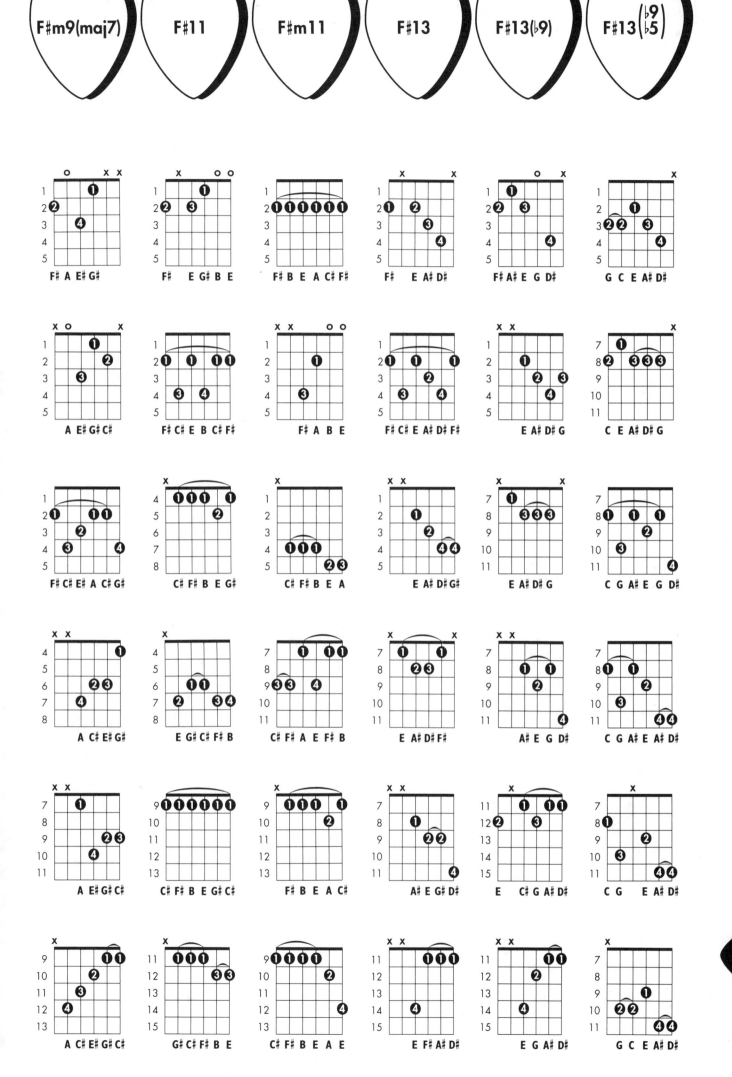

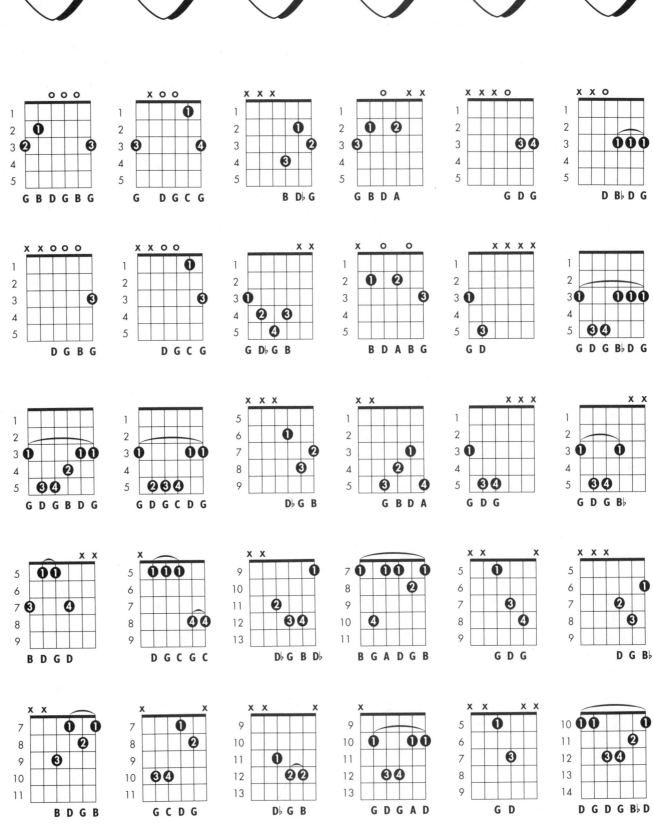

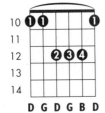 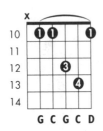 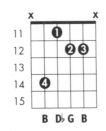 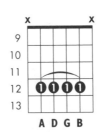 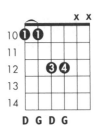 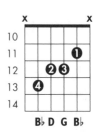

G

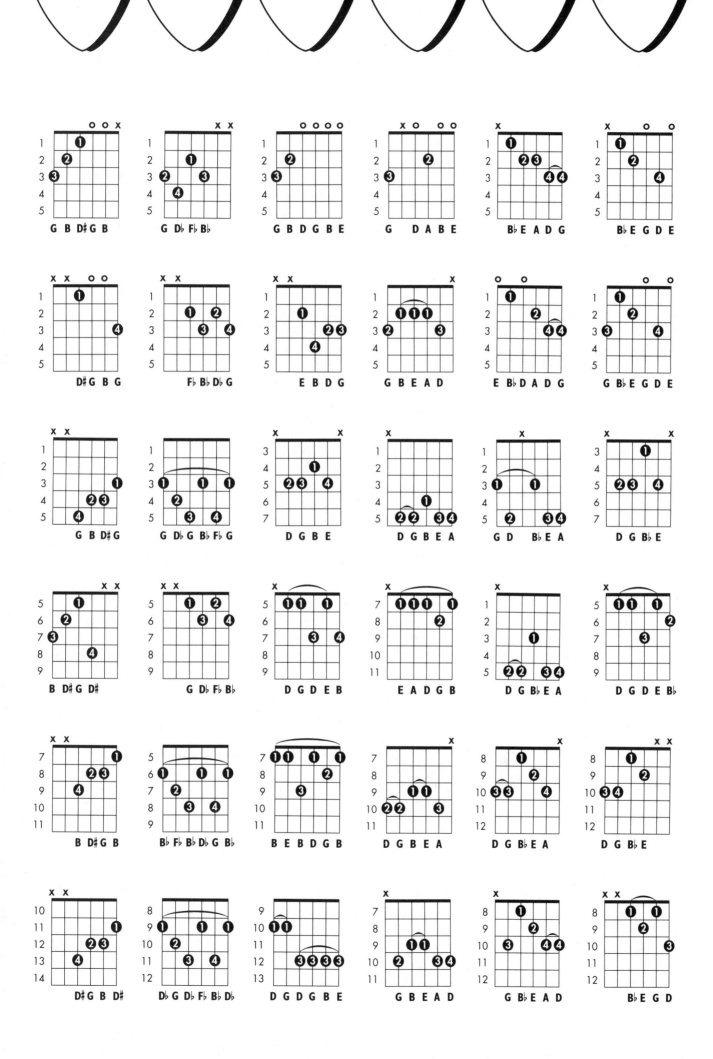

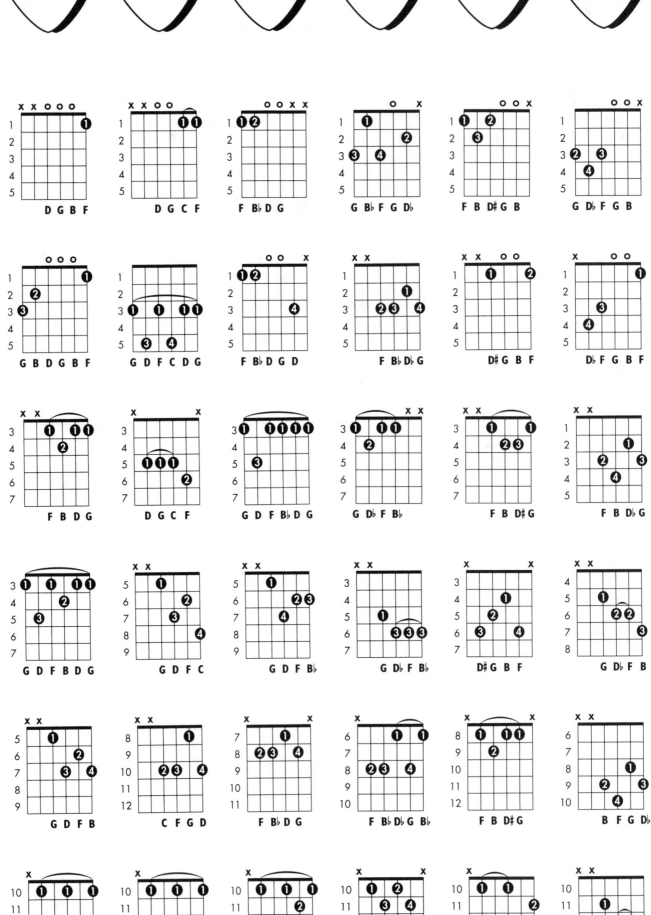

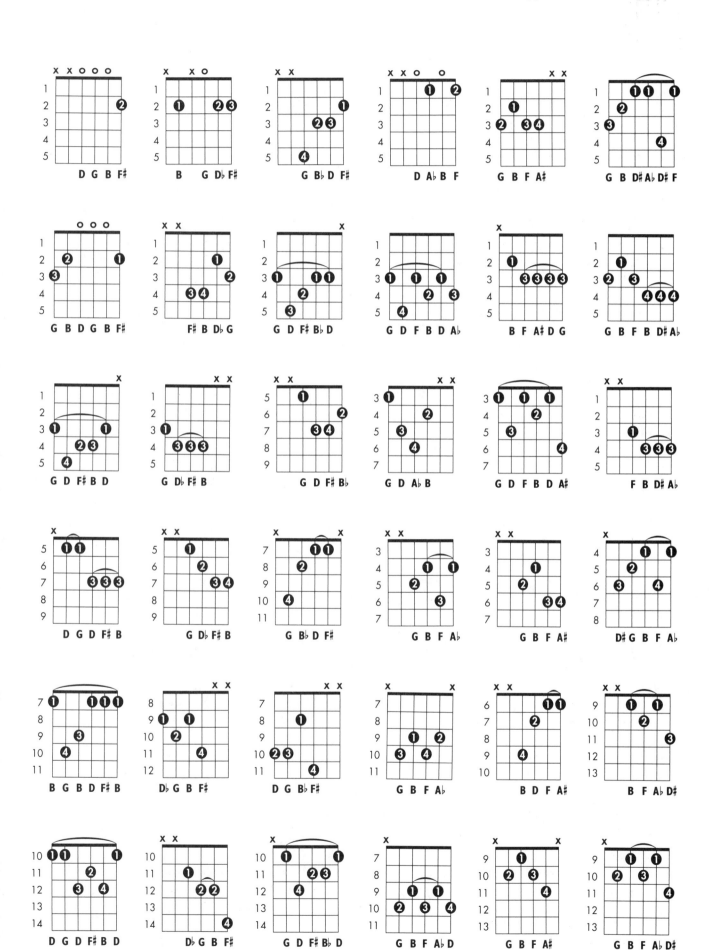

G

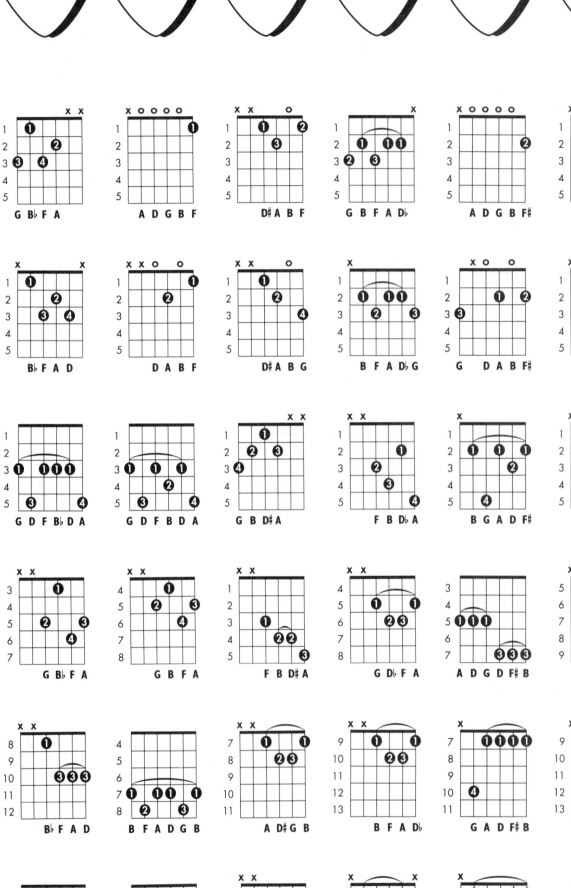

Gm9   **G9**   **G9+**   **G9(♭5)**   **Gmaj9**   **G9(#11)**

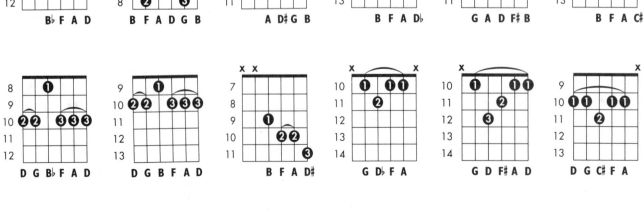

G

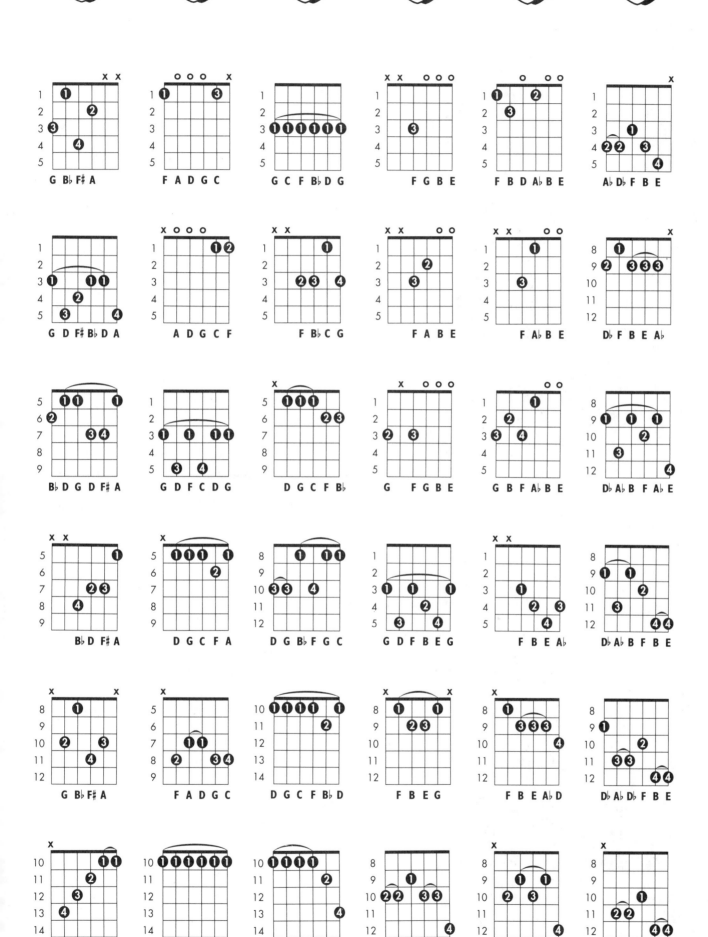

George Strait

George Strait is among the generation of performers who gave country music a new energy and popularity in the 1980s. His style recalls the honky-tonk sound of country music popular in the 1950s and has given him over 20 number-one hits.

Photo: Amy Lehman © 1995

Neil Finn (Crowded House)

*Along with his brother Tim, **Neil Finn** first found great success with the New Zealand-based band* Split Enz. *He later went on to form the highly successful group* Crowded House *in 1986. Both brothers were awarded the OBE in 1993 for their musical contributions to New Zealand.*

Photo: Amy Lehman © 1994

Tablature Explanation

Tablature is a system of notation that graphically represents the strings and frets of the guitar fingerboard. Each note is indicated by placing a number, which indicates the fret or finger position to be picked, on the appropriate string. For example:

1st String, 10th Fret
2nd String, 10th Fret] – Played together

4th String, 5th Fret

An open G chord

The musical examples outlined in this section explore different stylistic characteristics and are provided as a source of departure for further experimentation. All examples are written in conventional notation as well as tablature. The following explains four tablature symbols that are used in this section:

Palm Mute (P.M.):

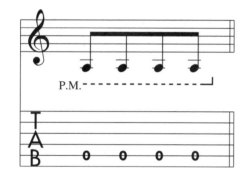

The note is partially muted by the pick hand by lightly touching the string or strings just before the bridge.

Slide:

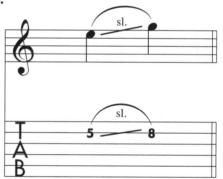

Pick the lower first note, then slide the fret finger up to sound the higher (second) note. The higher note is not picked again.

Pull-off:

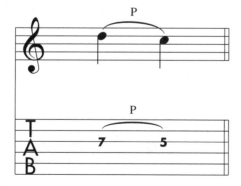

Place both fret fingers on the two notes to be played. Pick the higher (first) note, then pull-off (raise up) the finger of the higher note while keeping the lower note fretted. Pick only the first note.

Hammer-on:

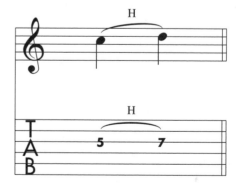

Pick the lower (first) note, then hammer-on (tap down) the higher (second) note with another finger. Pick only the first note. These notes are always played on the same string.

Track 1 (Tuning)

Track 2

1

Track 3

2

Blues

1 Track 4

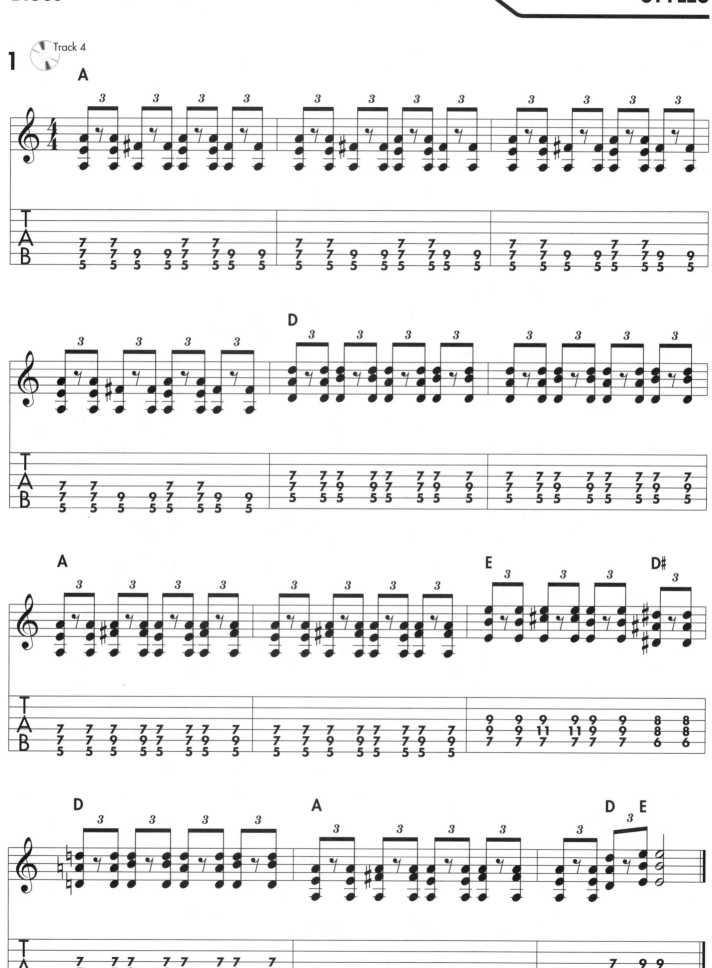

STYLES

2 Track 5

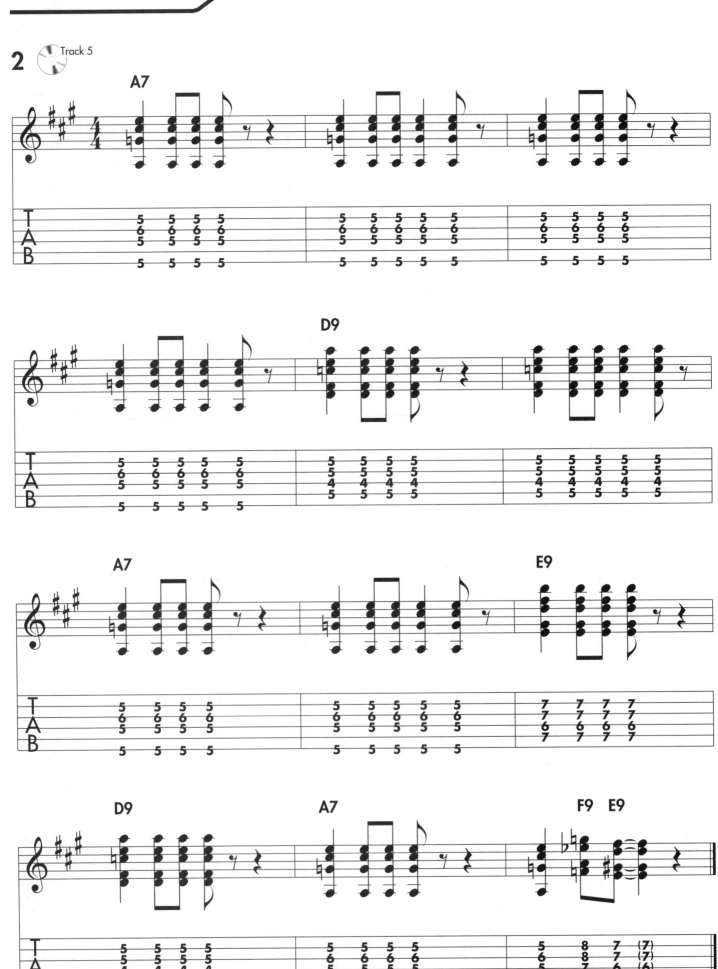

Buddy Guy

*A classic Chicago electric-bluesman, **Buddy Guy** came into prominence in the 1960s, and with his screaming Stratocaster style, became one of the blues' great ambassadors to rock audiences.*

Photo: Institute of Jazz Studies

STYLES

Funk

1 Track 8

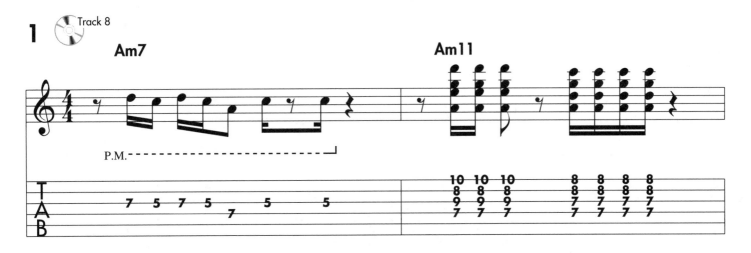

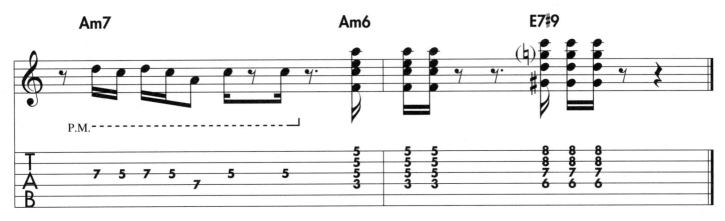

2 Track 9

1 Track 10

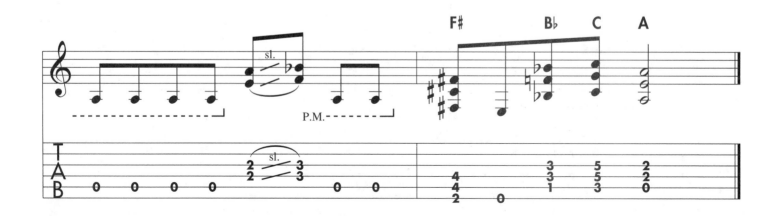

2 Track 11

Jazz

1 Track 12

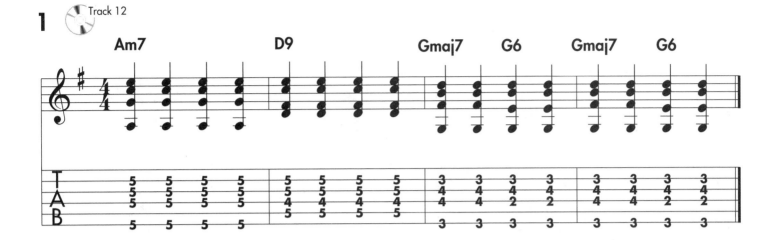

2 Track 13

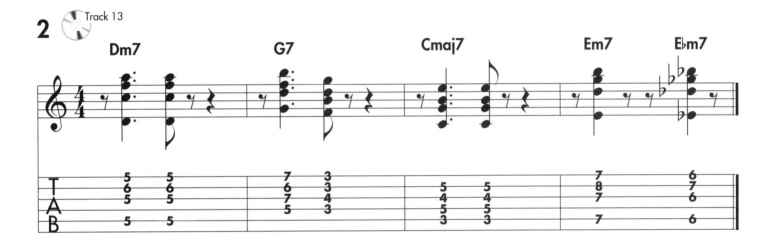

Allan Holdsworth

British guitarist **Allan Holdsworth** has pushed the boundaries of guitar playing, both with the progressive rock band UK, as well as with his own solo career. Eddie Van Halen is among his many fans.

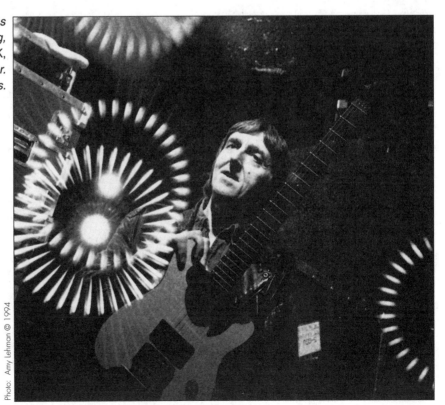

Photo: Amy Lehman © 1994

Reggae

1 Track 16

2 Track 17

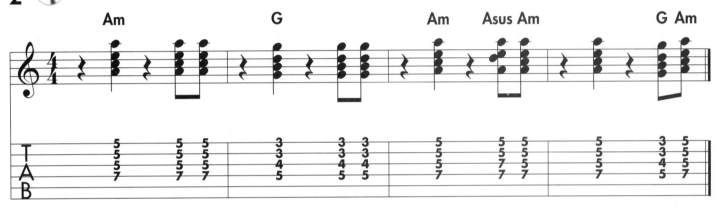

Bob Marley

Extending the evolution of musical styles from the West Indies such as calypso and ska, reggae came into prominence during the 1960s and, particularly, in the 1970s. **Bob Marley** *is a music legend, and one of the true founders of reggae.*

1  Track 18

2 Track 19

Rockabilly

1 Track 20

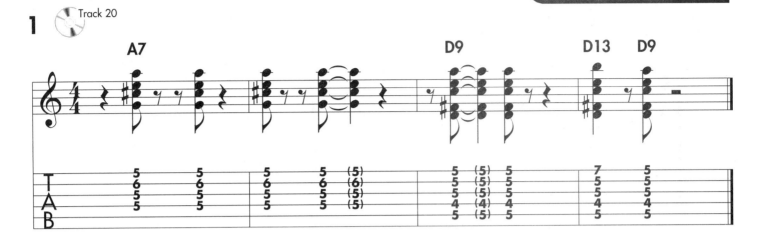

2 Track 21

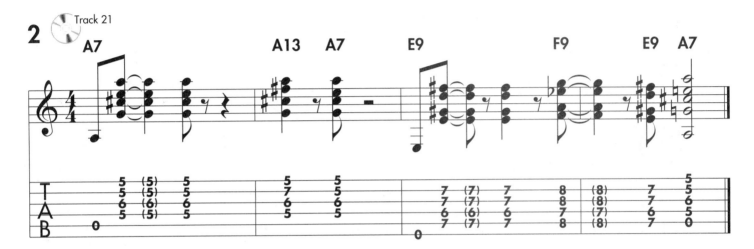

John Lennon

One of the giants of rock 'n' roll, from his first records with The Beatles *through his successful solo career,* **John Lennon** *played a major role in shaping pop music into what it is today. His combination of graceful melodies, unusual chord progressions and literate, sometimes biting, lyrics set a new standard for songwriting that continues to inspire fans around the world.*

Guitar Fingerboard Chart
Frets 1–12

STRINGS

6th 5th 4th 3rd 2nd 1st
E A D G B E

Fret	6th	5th	4th	3rd	2nd	1st
Open	E	A	D	G	B	E
1st Fret	F	A#/B♭	D#/E♭	G#/A♭	C	F
2nd Fret	F#/G♭	B	E	A	C#/D♭	F#/G♭
3rd Fret	G	C	F	A#/B♭	D	G
4th Fret	G#/A♭	C#/D♭	F#/G♭	B	D#/E♭	G#/A♭
5th Fret	A	D	G	C	E	A
6th Fret	A#/B♭	D#/E♭	G#/A♭	C#/D♭	F	A#/B♭
7th Fret	B	E	A	D	F#/G♭	B
8th Fret	C	F	A#/B♭	D#/E♭	G	C
9th Fret	C#/D♭	F#/G♭	B	E	G#/A♭	C#/D♭
10th Fret	D	G	C	F	A	D
11th Fret	D#/E♭	G#/A♭	C#/D♭	F#/G♭	A#/B♭	D#/E♭
12th Fret	E	A	D	G	B	E

Fingerboard diagram (string letter names per fret):

1st Fret: F B♭ E♭ A♭ C F (A# D# G#)

2nd Fret: F#/G♭ B E A D♭/G♭ (C#/F#)

3rd Fret: G C F B♭/A# D G

4th Fret: G#/A♭ C#/D♭ F#/G♭ B E♭/A♭ (D# G#)

5th Fret: A D G C E A

6th Fret: A#/B♭ E♭/D# G#/A♭ C#/D♭ F A#/B♭

7th Fret: B E A D G♭/F# B

8th Fret: C F B♭/A# E♭/D# G C

9th Fret: C#/D♭ F#/G♭ B E A♭/G# C#/D♭

10th Fret: D G C F A D

11th Fret: D#/E♭ G#/A♭ C#/D♭ F#/G♭ A#/B♭ D#/E♭

12th Fret: E A D G B E